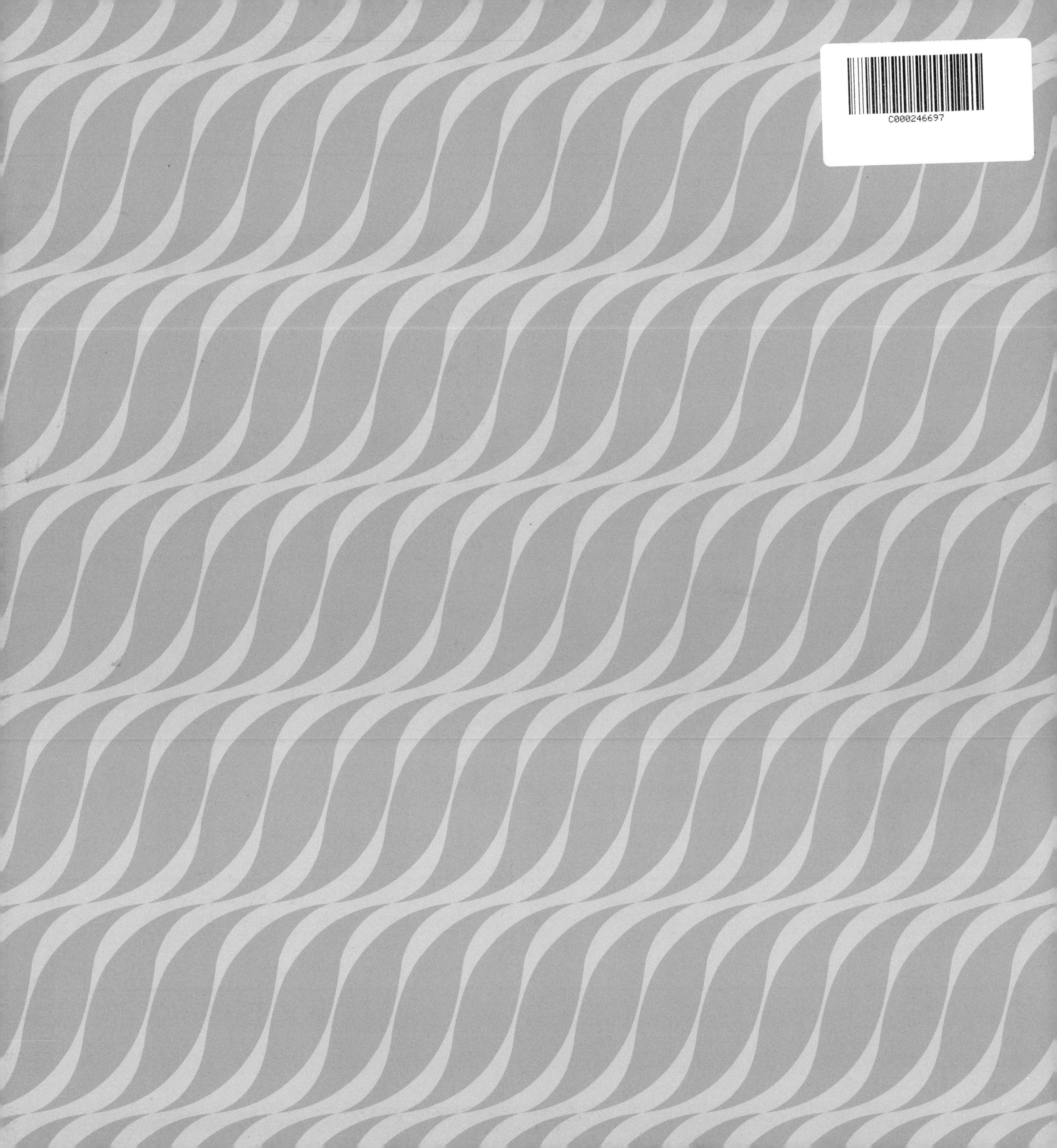
C000246697

CLASSIC
British CARS
A RETROSPECTIVE VIEW OF THE BRITISH AUTOMOBILE INDUSTRY
RBE 933

Abbeydale Press

CLASSIC British CARS

A RETROSPECTIVE VIEW OF THE BRITISH AUTOMOBILE INDUSTRY

Ian Ward

This edition is published by
Abbeydale Press,
an imprint of Anness Publishing Ltd,
Hermes House, 88–89 Blackfriars Road,
London SE1 8HA
tel. 020 7401 2077;
fax 020 7633 9499
www.annesspublishing.com

Anness Publishing has a new
picture agency outlet for images
for publishing, promotions or advertising.
Please visit our website
www.practicalpictures.com for
more information.

*Produced for Anness Publishing
Ltd by:* Editorial Developments,
Edgmond, Shropshire, England

Designer: Chensie Chen
Indexer: Quentin C Daniel

A CIP catalogue record for this book is
available from the British Library.

ETHICAL TRADING POLICY
Because of our ongoing ecological
investment programme, you, as our
customer, can have the pleasure and
reassurance of knowing that a tree
is being cultivated on your behalf to
naturally replace the materials used to
make the book you are holding.
For further information about this scheme,
go to *www.annesspublishing.com/trees*

CONTENTS

AC Ace & Cobra

Only a handful of enthusiasts will remember him today, but had it not been for gifted Portuguese-born engineer John Tojeiro, the beautiful AC Ace would probably never have existed – and would certainly not have been the car it was. Tojeiro was introduced to the Hurlock brothers, who owned AC Cars, in 1953, and he showed them his Bristol-engined special that had been raced with success by Cliff Davis. So impressed were Charles and William that they quickly did a deal with Tojeiro and the resultant Ace was unveiled at the London Motor Show later that year.

Now powered by the venerable 2-litre overhead-cam straight-six that had graced the worthy AC saloon for years, the production version of the Ace, as modified by Alan Turner, was if anything even sleeker and more handsome than the Tojeiro, with aluminium panelling forming a two-seat convertible body that

A large opening at the front of the Ace bodywork allows good airflow to pass to the radiator, in turn helping to cool the Bristol six-cylinder engine.

The simple but beautiful lines of the Ace, which used a light, ladder-style tubular frame designed by John Tojeiro.

The two-seater, alloy body style of the AC Ace was clearly inspired by the Ferrari barchetta of the period.

No lack of instruments on the Ace dashboard, keeping the driver informed of what is happening under the bonnet.

was mounted on a tubular steel chassis. As old as the engine was, it could propel the Ace to the magic "ton" and even a little beyond – not at all bad for the early 1950s. The lightweight body kept the centre of gravity low, so that cornering was flat and grip was good, helped by independent suspension all round in which transverse leaf springs doubled as upper wishbones.

Responding to customer demand, AC, based in Surrey's leafy Thames Ditton, made the BMW-based Bristol 2-litre engine an option in 1956 and with the top speed now up to 185 kph (115 mph), the inadequate drum front brakes gave way to discs. In tuned form, Aces achieved considerable competition success, not least at the Le Mans 24-hour race, which brought a class win and seventh overall in 1959.

The light-alloy AC engine was offered throughout the life of the Ace, but by 1961 Bristol was looking towards American V8 power for its own cars and AC took a lead from specialist tuner

The early Ace used the ageing AC 2-litre, overhead cam, 100-bhp, in-line, 6-cylinder engine, but from 1956 the option of Bristol's 2-litre 120 bhp in-line 6-cylinder engine (left) was also available. This came with three downdraft carburettors and four speed gearbox. For a short period a Ken Rudd "Ruddspeed" Ford engine was also available.

Ken Rudd in adopting the 2.6-litre Ford Zephyr straight-six in place of the Bristol unit. Being bigger and heavier, the Ford engine demanded a re-worked bonnet and beefed-up suspension. In fact, only around 47 such Aces were turned out during the next two years, but the uprating opened the way for what was to follow.

American racer Carroll Shelby wanted to build a lightweight sports car powered by a lusty V8 engine and capable of rivalling Ferraris and Chevrolet Corvettes on the track. Despite its long and distinguished production history, AC also had an engineering heritage and the company remained small and flexible enough to accommodate a request from Shelby to modify its Ace to accept

The Cobra had an extensive and successful racing career under Carroll Shelby. He wanted it to be a Corvette beater and being some 500 pounds (227 kg) lighter, it did just that.

Probably one of the most desired sports cars ever, the Cobra needs no introduction. It has all the ingredients that any sportscar driver would want – big engine with lots of power, matched to a well designed chassis and sporting body.

a "small-block" Ford V8. The project was supported by Ford, which supplied one of its new lightweight 260 cu in, or 4.2-litre units to the factory.

The conversion proved remarkably trouble-free. The steering box had to be moved and a new arrangement made to accommodate a Salisbury limited-slip differential – as used by Jaguars – but other modifications were minor. The prototype also had inboard rear disc brakes, another Jaguar feature, but these were shifted to the conventional position next to the wheels in production models. The wheels themselves were widened and covered by a subtle lip around each wheelarch and the radiator grille was enlarged.

This was the Cobra. The prototype was air-freighted to the USA early in 1962 and production was soon under way. AC would send unpowered cars to California, where Shelby's race shop would install the engines and complete final assembly.

In fact, interest was such that the 100 cars required for homologation to realise Carroll Shelby's racing ambitions were soon built – the company was to become the champion World

Sports Car Manufacturer in 1965. Even in road trim, the pace of the Cobra was very lively, with a top speed of around 209 kph (130 mph) and surprisingly nimble handling, thanks to the engine being mounted well back in the chassis.

With 75 Cobras built, a bigger Ford engine, with a 289 cu in (4.7-litre) capacity was introduced and with 271 bhp top speed went up to nearly 225 kph (140 mph) and a 0–100 kph (0–60 mph) time of 5.5 seconds (variants were listed with up to 300 bhp). Fifty cars later, the old worm-and-sector steering box was replaced by sensitive and direct rack-and-pinion steering.

Always looking for more performance to vanquish racing opposition, Carroll Shelby shoe-horned Ford's mighty 427 cu in (7-litre) V8 into the chassis, which now had coil spring suspension and enlarged tubes, for 1965. The elegance and grace of the Ace body had by now been compromised with bulging wheel arches and ultra-fat tyres, but this gave the Cobra its own appeal as a true muscle car, with a top speed on the plus side of 257 kph (160 mph). Some cars, confusingly, had a completely different but similarly sized Ford 428 cu in engine, even though the model was still known as the 427.

Shelby production ceased in 1966, although AC continued to build Cobras for another three years. Things had moved on and the shortcomings of the primitive chassis were no longer acceptable in a car with so much power. Shelby, too, moved on to build Ford Mustang-derived Cobras and production ended with just under 1000 of the ACs produced. The story of the AC marque has since been distinctly chequered and various "new" versions of the Cobra have appeared, including a sophisticated carbon-fibre based MkIV, but none has seen serious production and it is largely left to the replica makers to keep the glorious shape alive.

AC Cobra 1963

Engine type	V8, ohv
Power	271 bhp (gross) @ 6000 rpm
Bore/stroke	101.6 x 72.9 mm (4.00 x 2.87 in)
Capacity	4728cc (289 cu in)
Transmission	Rear drive, four gears
Wheelbase	2290 mm (90 in)
Top speed	216 kph (135 mph)

Comprehensive instrumentation gave the driver peace of mind and allowed him to keep an eye on the functionality of the mechanics.

No doubts about the origins of this engine – seen here is one bank of the big V8, 4.2 litre powerplant, used in this early Cobra.

The twin chrome mini bumpers look a little like a set of teeth and the wide radiator grille a mouth, giving the cobra a menacing look from the front end. Controlling it can be a little scary if you don't have your wits about you. The power is extraordinary and the noise alone is enough to send shivers up your back.

The stubby, 4-speed gearshift. The little "T" shaped handle just below the knob is pulled up when selecting reverse gear.

Alvis T-series sixes

For a company with such a distinguished name, Alvis had a remarkably chequered history. Founded in 1920, the business survived receivership four years later and went on to build some of the finest British cars, not least the six-cylinder T-series that was unveiled as the TA 21 in 1950 and, in TF 21 form, was the last car produced by the company in 1967.

In fact, Alvis never built a complete car. Bodies were always supplied by specialist coachbuilders and a number of these provided clothes for the T-series, which marked a return to the upper end of the motor car market. The company did, however, manufacture its own engines and in this case power came from a 3-litre straight-six. A long-stroke unit, whose dimensions did not change throughout the model's life, this was a simple

Seen here is a well-preserved TA 21, but with non-standard wire wheels. Many owners fitted these to their cars, thus giving them a sportier look.

The Alvis TC 21 model range was introduced in 1953, replacing the similar TA 21. The TC 21/100 Grey Lady was the high performance version of this range and was instantly distinguished by the wire wheels and two air scoops strategically placed on the top of the bonnet.

A chrome strip shows off the smooth line of the boot; a lockable, twist-type handle gives access to the boot area; the Alvis badge is strategically placed just below it.

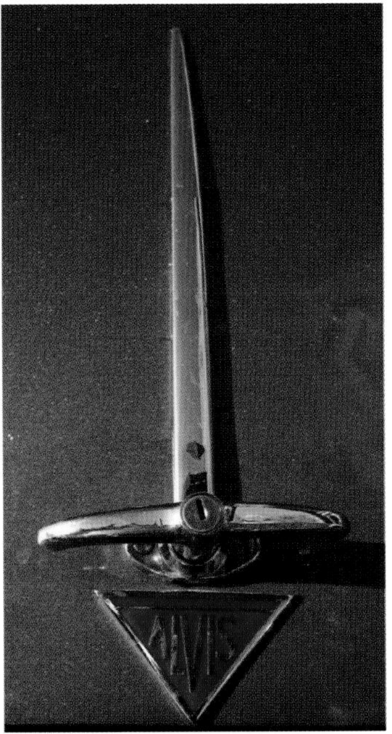

pushrod design, albeit one in which the pushrods were gently sprung against the rockers to minimise noise. With a single Solex carburettor, power was a modest 90 bhp and this was passed to the leaf-sprung rear axle via Alvis's own four-speed gearbox. Front suspension was independent, with wishbones and coil springs, and telescopic dampers were fitted all round, as were hydraulic drum brakes. The chassis was a substantial steel box-section affair, which was both lighter and more rigid than in earlier cars.

With only around the same power output as some of the company's earlier and smaller engines, the TA was never going to win any outright performance prizes with a top speed of around 145 kph (90 mph), but it was noted for its smoothness, quietness and mid-range pulling power. Body style played a part in determining this and there were two "standard" options for the TA. Mulliner made a four-door saloon, complete with sunroof and lightweight aluminium door frames and pillars, while a two-door convertible was produced by Tickford. Some chassis were despatched to Switzerland, where sleek and elegant coachwork was added by Hermann Graber, who was to play a big part later in the T-series story.

Twin SU carburettors soon replaced the Solex and further improved the engine's manners, although a larger single SU graced some examples of the TB 21 sports two-seater that appeared in 1951. The AP Metalcraft bodywork was modified from that fitted to the earlier TB 14, with a traditional grille in place of the 14's avant garde offering.

Alvis prices might have been lower than those of Rolls-Royce, but these were hand-built quality cars, aimed at the discerning well-to-do enthusiast, and factory output was always distinctly modest. Only some 20 TB 21s were made, for instance, while

Seen from the rear, the Grey Lady looked curvaceous and quite sporty for a rather upright looking saloon.

The TC range was produced between 1953 and 1955 and some 757 examples were manufactured during that period.

total production of the TA and the TC that followed was a little over 2,000.

That TC, introduced in 1953, differed little from the TA, being distinguished by such niceties as concealed door hinges. This did nothing to arrest falling demand for a now dated model until a power boost brought by a new camshaft and improved carburation was standardised and a revised name reflected the top speed that was now possible. Soon nicknamed the Grey Lady, the TC 21/100, with 104 bhp on tap and with wire wheels and bonnet louvres as common distinguishing marks, gained favourable publicity with its magic "ton" capability, and sales were soon on the up, although the boost was to be short-lived.

In 1954, Mulliner was taken over by Standard, and with Tickford now owned by Aston Martin body supply was suddenly a major problem. By this time, car production was becoming something of a side-line for Alvis, which now had a well-established business making aero-engines and armoured vehicles – something that was just as well given the car side's losses. Yet the company did not give up. It turned once again to Graber, which designed a graceful and altogether more modern two-door body for what was to be known as the TC 108G. Lower and stiffer than its predecessors, this performed and handled better and was arguably the most attractive car ever made by the company. The

Two vents, positioned just behind the grille on either side of the bonnet, give better ventilation to the engine and its compartment.

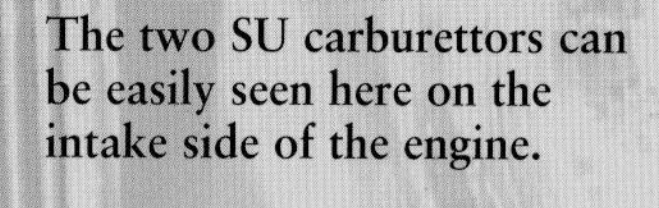

The two SU carburettors can be easily seen here on the intake side of the engine.

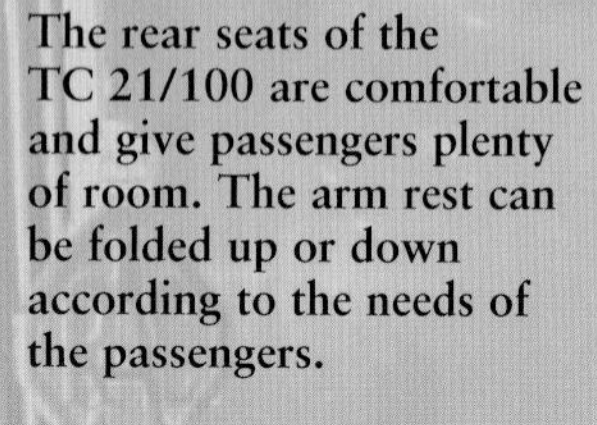

The rear seats of the TC 21/100 are comfortable and give passengers plenty of room. The arm rest can be folded up or down according to the needs of the passengers.

In 1964 Alvis up-dated its coupé model with the more powerful TE 21. Although the styling of the car remained similar to its predecessor, stacked headlights gave the front-end a clean and elegant look, along with its long slim radiator.

Alvis TC21/100
1953

Engine type	In-line six-cylinder, ohc
Power	104 bhp @ 4000 rpm
Bore/stroke	84 x 90 mm (3.31 x 3.54 in)
Capacity	2993cc (182 cu in)
Transmission	Rear drive, four gears
Wheelbase	2830 mm (111.5 in)
Top speed	160 kph (100 mph)

The long bonnet of the TE 21 gave the car a streamlined look. Under it lurked a powerful, 3-litre, 6-cylinder, 130 bhp engine, which would happily power the car to a smooth and comfortable 142 kph (89 mph).

Although a convertible, the long chassis enabled the car to have a good boot area. An ideal touring car, it had plenty of room for luggage.

body tooling was brought to England and installed at bus coachbuilder Willowbrook, but prices were very high and sales almost non-existent and car production was almost at a standstill until 1958 when the combined Mulliner Park Ward, now part of Rolls-Royce, re-worked the body to provide better accommodation.

This was the TD 21, which had options of two-door saloon or drop-head styles. A new cylinder head pushed power up to 120 bhp, with front disc brakes installed to match the improved performance. Automatic transmission was also now an option, as was overdrive for the Austin-Healey derived manual box. A Mark II version came in 1962, with all-round discs and aluminium doors, while a ZF five-speed gearbox was soon a standard item.

Sales rocketed and by the time the TE 21 appeared early in 1964 over 1000 TDs had been made. Four headlamps distinguished the new model, big valves and a matching exhaust increased power to 130 bhp and speed to 180 kph (112 mph). Power steering was added the following year and some 350 TEs were produced, some with bespoke Graber bodies.

The end of the line came in 1966 with the TF. This looked the same, but triple SUs and a compression ratio increase had brought the power output to 150 bhp and coaxed 193 kph (120 mph) top speed out of the car. Again, Graber made some of the 100 or so examples, for those with extra funds at their disposal, but by now Alvis was part of the ill-starred British Leyland empire and car production was halted for ever in 1967.

Looking a little Art Deco'ish, this is the stylish handle which allows access to the boot area.

Big instruments and lots of room to relax behind the steering wheel, the TE is a pleasure to drive even for long distances.

Aston Martin DB4–6

The DB years were some of the most vital in the chequered history of Aston Martin. The company saw a long period of relative stability under the stewardship of (Sir) David Brown, whose initials the cars bore.

The 2-litre, retrospectively dubbed the DB1, was already under development when Brown bought the company early in 1947 and brought Lagonda into the fold later that year. It was the existence of a superior WO Bentley-designed Lagonda engine that did for the DB1 after only 14 had been constructed, powering the all-new DB2 of 1950. This car and its variants did well for the company on and off the track for the next eight years, with 1726 cars sold, but as early as 1954 work was under way on an exciting new model that was to be different from the ground up.

This was the DB4 (DB3 had been a racer). As originally designed by Harold Beach, this had a steel perimeter frame on which were mounted coil spring and wishbone independent front

The Aston Martin 2-litre Sports, retrospectively known as the DB1, was shown at the London Motor Show in 1948. It was a direct descendant of the earlier prototype known as the "Atom".

One of three DB2s sent straight from production to the Aston Martin racing department for conversion, which were due to compete in the 1950 Le Mans 24-hour race.

suspension and a de Dion rear axle arrangement with trailing links and torsion bar springs. The first body, a traditional closed type, was styled by Frank Feeley and power responsibilities remained with the DB2's straight-six in slightly enlarged 3-litre form.

The project meandered without much apparent direction for a couple of years, but with John Wyer (later to be famous for his legendary Gulf Ford and Gulf Porsche Le Mans cars) taking on the roles of Technical Director and General Manager alongside his duties as Competitions Manager, a new impetus was gained.

Shown here is the hatchback style rear end of the DB2/4, which also made its way onto the DB Mark III coupe. The DB2/4 was produced between 1953 and 1957 and some 764 were made. The two Italian styling companies Bertone and Touring also produced "Spider" versions of the car.

Only fifteen DB1 models were sold between 1948 and 1950 and it featured many of the novelties found in the Atom, most importantly its chassis and lightweight body construction.

The first decision was to ditch the old power plant in favour of a purpose-built twin-overhead-cam straight-six from the pen of Polish engineer Tadek Marek, who had joined Aston Martin in 1954. With "square" bore and stroke dimensions of 92 mm, this sturdy 3670cc engine had an aluminium cylinder head and, by the time production started, an aluminium block. Breathing through twin SU carburettors, it developed 240 bhp at 5750 rpm.

With power taken care of, attention turned to the body. Wyer was not happy with the worthy but somewhat dull prototype shell, so he looked to Carrozzeria Touring Superleggera, of Milan, to inject some Italian flair into the package. But there was a snag. On seeing the blueprints, the styling house politely declined the invitation, pointing out that the chassis was not suited to its hallmark Superleggera (super-lightweight) construction, which consisted of an aluminium-alloy skin wrapped around a framework of narrow tubes.

A beautiful example of a DB Mark III and one of only a handful of convertibles made. Production went from 1957 through 1959. The car was an evolution of the DB2/4 Mark II model, which it replaced.

The power unit of the DB4 – a double overhead camshaft, 3.7-litre, in-line 6-cylinder engine that produced around 240 bhp. The car had rapid acceleration and a top speed of 224 kph (140 mph).

Designer Beach was undeterred and within a few weeks he had penned a new platform chassis to match Touring's requirements, the first example being despatched to Italy for a body to be fitted. The completed car was put through its paces first by David Brown and then on a long continental excursion by John Wyer. Both pronounced themselves happy with this sleek fastback two-plus-two, despite a list of minor faults and complaints. One major change made before production began at the end of 1958 was to ditch the de Dion rear end, with its overly noisy final drive, in favour of a live axle arrangement, with coil springs and a Watts linkage to supplement the trailing arms.

The DB4 was enthusiastically received by the press, which was just as well because it was considerably more expensive than the DB Mark III that it replaced. It was beautifully finished and equipped and its performance reflected its lightweight construction and

DAVID BROWN
ASTON MARTIN

The new 4-seater bodywork of the Aston Martin DB4 was styled by Touring of Milan, Italy and constructed around their patented "Superleggera" steel frame and mounted to a steel platform chassis – the DB4 was quite different from any of the previous Aston Martin models.

Superleggera

Aston Martin DB4
1959

Engine type	In-line six-cylinder, ohc
Power	240 bhp @ 5750 rpm
Bore/stroke	92 x 92 mm (3.62 x 3.62 in)
Capacity	3670cc (224 cu in)
Transmission	Rear drive, four gears
Wheelbase	2490 mm (98 in)
Top speed	224 kph (140 mph)

its smooth shape, with a top speed of around 225 kph (140 mph). Over the next couple of years, modifications were plentiful, some to cure problems and others to improve the breed by way of evolution. The gearbox was improved, oil consumption was reduced, the all-round disc brakes were uprated and a twin-plate clutch replaced the original single-plate item, while faired-in headlamps improved both the look and the aerodynamics.

Those headlamps had first appeared on the uprated Vantage edition. With a raised compression ratio, this had 20 more bhp and a performance boost to match. For the ultimate from this model, buyers could turn to the DB4 GT. With three Weber carburettors taking power to 302 bhp and nearly 90.7 kg (200 lb) pared from its mass, thanks to a shorter, lighter two-seat body, the GT could top 241 kph (150 mph). The Dunlop brakes were ousted by the more effective Girlings that would grace all future DBs in this series. A few GT chassis were sent to Zagato in Milan, where the lightest, most slippery and supremely muscular body of all coupled with a high-compression 314 bhp engine to push the speed potential to an amazing 257 kph (160 mph).

A version of the DB4 produced by the Italian styling company Zagato. The aggressively styled GTZ had a lightweight body and thus was used mainly for racing. These are rare collectors' cars today.

Although the DB4 was developed through five distinctive versions, many were also modified for specific racing situations. Not specifically designed to race but who could resist driving this baby!

The DB4GT (left) was a heavy and well-equipped car and even though lighter and with a shorter wheelbase than the DB4, the two-seater was just not suitable for the track. The beautifully presented 3.7 litre, 6-cylinder engine pushed out 302 bhp at 6000 rpm (right).

Sales of the DB4 were undoubtedly helped by success on the track, in the hands of drivers such as Stirling Moss. Of the 1110 examples sold, 75 were GTs, 19 were Zagatos and 70 were drop-heads, this model having first appeared in 1961. In fact the Zagato story was not over because six officially sanctioned further examples were built in the 1990s, under the direction of specialist Richard Williams, using left-over chassis numbers and modifications to suit modern times and to iron out minor irritations.

The faults of the DB4 were all addressed in the DB5 of 1963. Most notable were improvements to the engine, which had now been enlarged to 3995cc by adding 4 mm to the bore. This now drove the rear wheels through a five-speed ZF gearbox but some of the extra power (282 bhp in all) was absorbed by the additional weight of equipment such as adjustable dampers, air conditioning and electric windows. The Vantage version was also uprated to develop 314 bhp. The convertible was now known as the Volante, a name that was to stick for the future, and 125 of

The double overhead camshaft, 6-cylinder, 3995 cc engine (243.8 cu in) (left) was matched to a four-speed gearbox, to give the car a top speed in excess of 224 kph (140 mph). The 0 to 96 kph (60 mph) figure was given as 8.1 seconds.

Any James Bond film addict will remember *Goldfinger*, which brought the DB5 to the attention of the general public and made it an overnight celebrity. Both the coupe (left) and the newly named Volante convertible (top) had increased power, beautiful interior and exterior styling and of course plenty of comfort (above).

The DB6 was introduced just two years after the DB5 and the front end took a similar shape to its predecessor, as can be seen with these inlaid headlights with their transparent covers.

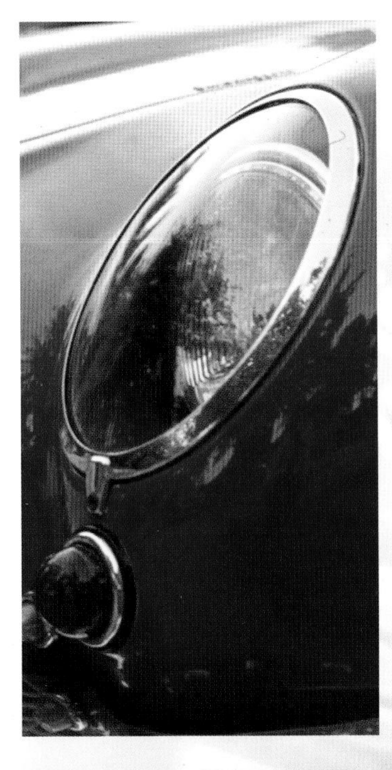

the 1025 DB5s were such models. There were even 12 estate cars, produced by coachbuilder Harold Radford.

The most famous DB5 of all was that belonging to James Bond in the film Goldfinger. Supposedly equipped with all sorts of gadgets dreamed up by "Q", such as machine guns, rotating number plates, a bullet-proof rear screen and an ejector seat, this was certainly one of the most popular Corgi toys made.

Late in 1965, the DB5 was joined in the range for the last months of its life by the longer-wheelbase DB6. This had increased rear passenger space, due partly to the stretched chassis and partly to an extended roof line. It could easily be identified by its kicked-up spoiler tail, apparently introduced to aid high-speed stability. The interior was also updated for the first time since 1958. Automatic transmission was by now an option, and limited-slip differential and chrome wire wheels were standard, but mechanical changes were minimal and the small performance increase was due to the aerodynamic improvements.

If the front had similarities to the DB5, the rear of the DB6 was very different. Not only was the car lengthened to give more room inside, but it also received a new Kamm-style tail treatment, which helped with stability at high speed. The beautiful Volante drophead (above) was introduced one year after the 2+2 (below).

The initial Volante version was an interim model built on the DB5 chassis but with the DB6 tail. A year later, this gave way to a "proper" DB6 Volante, complete with the longer wheelbase and a power-operated hood for the first time.

Similar though the DB6 looked to the DB5, the Superleggera construction had been replaced by a more conventional aluminium body and steel floor pan, Touring having fallen on hard times in 1966. A MkII version was announced in 1969, with larger wheels and tyres and wheel arches flared to accommodate them. The interior was updated again and there was now an option of Brico fuel injection for the engine.

The DB6 was made alongside the new and very different DBS for a couple of years, but in 1970, this distinguished line came to an end, with 1575 DB6 models having left the factory.

Austin Seven

If the board of Austin had had its way, the company's world famous baby might never have been born. After the First World War, Sir Herbert Austin, who had been knighted in 1917 when his factory was engaged in war work, decided to emulate Henry Ford and concentrate on a single car model. Unfortunately, the 3.6-litre Twenty of 1919 was not the car with which to catch the public's imagination and by 1921 a receiver was overseeing the company's activities on behalf of its creditors. A down-sized version of the Twenty, known as the Twelve, was pushed through by Austin, and reversed the fortunes of his business, but he now realised that diversity was essential and he began to look at adding a small car to the range.

The Austin Seven was one of the most popular cars ever produced, its popularity helping to eliminate many other British small cars and cyclecars of the period. It was also produced under licence by many foreign countries, of which the "Dixie" from German manufacturer BMW was one. In France they were made and sold by the Rosengart Company, while in Japan Nissan also used the design as the basis for their early cars.

There was little need for too much instrumentation. The whole idea of this car was that it was simple but functional and sold at a price that people could afford.

Sir Herbert's vision of a best-selling low-cost car that would take over from motor cycle combinations and cycle cars was not shared by his co-directors, so he seconded an eighteen-year-old draughtsman called Stanley Edge to work at his home on this new, and secret, project. Young Edge's first, and thankfully successful, task was to talk his boss out of fitting a lightweight twin-cylinder engine.

Austin himself penned the simple A-frame chassis and the neat and simple open-topped body that covered it. Edge's engine was a side-valve four, with two roller bearings for the crankshaft and a capacity of just 696cc, giving it an RAC rating (calculated from engine size rather than measured) of 7.2 hp – the actual figure was just under 10 bhp. Edge's chosen gear-box had three speeds and it drove a rear axle that was located on two quarter-elliptic leaf springs. No dampers were fitted and at the front a single transverse leaf spring looked after suspension. Four-wheel brakes were a real innovation for such a tiny car, but they were notably ineffective, the pedal acting on the rear and the handbrake on the front.

With the drawings completed in Sir Herbert's billiard room, it was time to begin construction. Such was the secrecy that an area of the works was partitioned off while the first three cars were put together between Easter and Whitsun of 1922. That initial trio differed slightly from each other in their propeller shaft arrangements, the version adopted for production being part open and part enclosed.

Revealed to the press in July, the Seven was well received by some but ridiculed by others for its size. It weighed only around

Austin Seven 1923

Engine type	In-line four cylinder, side valves
Power	10.5 bhp (gross) @ 2400 rpm
Bore/stroke	56 x 76.2 mm (2.2 x 3.0 in)
Capacity	747cc (45.6 cu in)
Transmission	Rear drive, three gears
Wheelbase	1900 mm (75 in)
Top speed	64 kph (40 mph)

The Austin Seven is often compared with the Ford Model T. It is a smaller car and weighs half that of the model T, thus it had a smaller engine to pull it along. Although it had brakes on all four wheels, they were only coupled in 1930. Lighting of course was less than adequate.

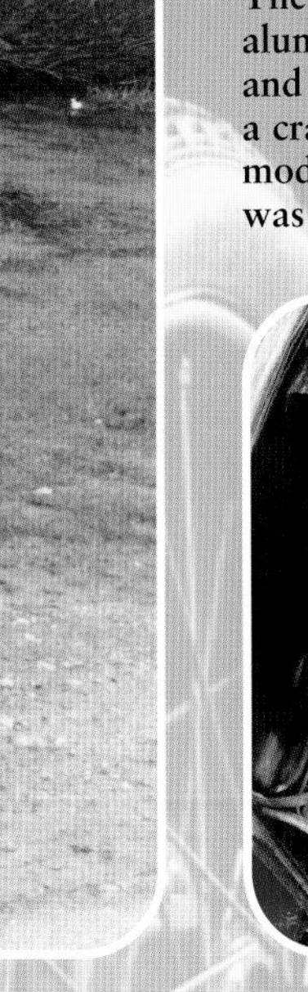

The four-cylinder engine was made up of an aluminium crankcase, a cast iron cylinder block and a cast iron cylinder head. Early engines had a crankshaft that ran in two bearings whilst later models went to three. In 1923 an electric starter was also added.

The controls found in the centre of the Seven steering wheel are common of cars up until the war period. The left lever, marked ignition, changes the timing from retarded to advanced, which means it alters at which point on the cylinder stroke the magneto produces a spark – one would normally start in a more retarded position and move to advanced when running. The "gas" lever is effectively a hand throttle and actuates on the same lever as the throttle pedal, and so enables slow running.

The Austin Seven Swallow Saloon had a bright two-tone colour scheme, with styling that was associated with more expensive cars of the time. Approximately 3500 bodies of various styles were produced up until 1932 when Lyons started making complete cars under the "SS" brand name. So much in demand were these little cars that in 1928, Lyons had to move production from Blackpool to Coventry. And thus laying down the foundation stone for what would become Jaguar Cars in 1945.

William Lyons, co-founder of the Swallow Sidecar Company, saw the commercial potential of producing a rebodied Austin Seven and so he commissioned coachbuilder Cyril Holland to produce a distinctive open tourer which would become the very successful Austin Seven Swallow. Because of its popularity, it wasn't long before it was followed, in 1928, by a saloon version, the Austin Seven Swallow Saloon.

330 kg (6.5 cwt), so that even with its modest muscle power it could manage nearly 64 kph (40 mph). A nominal four-seater, the car was not intended to carry a full complement of adults. The rear seat was clearly made for children.

Despite a price tag of £165, this novelty did not catch on straight away. Only 1936 Sevens were made in 1923, during which time a number of improvements were added. The engine capacity was increased to 748cc, giving 10.5 bhp (7.8 hp on the RAC scale on which tax was based), a cooling fan was fitted and a mechanical under-bonnet starting lever gave way to an electric starter.

It seems unlikely for such a puny contraption, but racing success was instrumental in building demand. The already noted aviator EC Gordon England challenged Austin to make him a racing version of the Seven before his leg, broken in a flying accident, healed. Sir Herbert was opposed to the idea of putting his baby into competition, but he could not resist the challenge and built a special chassis that with Gordon England's own lightweight body rewarded him by taking several records at Brooklands. Many competition variants and numerous noteworthy victories followed, a supercharged version becoming the first 750cc car to exceed 160 kph (100 mph). Austin was convinced and soon began making his own sporting versions of the Seven, the road-going Nippy of 1934 being among the most famous of these.

In 1924, sales accelerated, with 4600 cars built, and by 1926 the Seven had become a real best-seller. Body styles were numerous, some with individual names, such as the famous Chummy tourer, and specialist coachbuilders provided their own

interpretations. The Swallow Sidecar Company, which was in time to become Jaguar, produced probably the most handsome of these, styled by founder William Lyons himself. Sevens were also made under licence by several overseas manufacturers and copied by Nissan in Japan. Commercial variants were plentiful and there was even a single-seat racer. In fact just about every body style graced that simple chassis.

Improvements continued to be made throughout the car's life, although the price remained remarkably stable and so made the Seven an ever more attractive proposition. An extra 152 mm (6 in) in the wheelbase finally made the baby Austin a practical four-seater in 1932, while a year later a fourth, lower, ratio was added to the gearbox. A 900cc Big Seven was produced from 1937 alongside the then standard Ruby version of the little car and was a big seller for a year or so.

When time eventually caught up with the Seven in January 1939, over a quarter of a million examples had been built. The engine, which spawned a racing class, continued as the basis for Reliant's three-wheeler power plant until 1962. This was a truly remarkable car.

The whole Austin range received a make-over during 1934, including the Seven. The bonnet was made longer and the radiator was now placed under the cowl; even the spare wheel was neatly enclosed with a metal cover. Two years later several more modifications were made, such as increasing the power output, which would see the little car remain as popular as ever. It was now designated Mk II and this guise was to continue until production ceased in early 1939.

The late little Seven Ruby, was stacked with instrumentation, quite a contrast from the first examples that rolled off the production line and a sign of how fast the motor industry was moving at that time.

Austin Healey 100 & 3000

Cornish-born Donald Healey had been building cars in small numbers for a few years in the late 1940s when he realised that if his company was to succeed against tough opposition on both sides of the Atlantic, he would need a faster, lighter and, above all, cheaper model. He decided to build a two-seat sports car and to power it with the 2.6-litre ohv four from the Austin Atlantic. As it turned out, this was a wise choice. He arranged with Austin boss Sir Leonard Lord for this unit and running gear from the A90 to be supplied and then, with son Geoffrey, set about finalising the concept. The attractive and modern open body was designed by the company's own Gerry Coker, and the prototype shell was constructed by Tickford before the completed car was put through its paces for the first time.

A beautifully restored and lovingly looked after Austin Healey 100/6. This BN4, 6-port head model left the factory in Abingdon in January of 1958. This car carries build number 396 and the current owner acquired it in 1978. It went through a complete rebuild which was finished in 1984. It's a real show stopper and has won a number of concours events.

Overdrive was added to what was now a three-speed gear-box to ensure that the new Healey 100 would have the top speed to live up to its name. However, other changes were few before the new model was revealed to the public at the 1952 Earls Court Motor Show. By this time Austin and Morris had merged to become the British Motor Corporation and new BMC chief Leonard Lord was on the lookout for a sports car with which to conquer the US market. He had already commissioned prototypes from within the organisation and from Jensen and Frazer Nash, but on seeing the clamour at the 100's debut, he quickly did a deal with Donald Healey for his sports car to be the first BMC product – badged as the Austin Healey 100 by the time the show ended.

The economies of mass production meant that the price could be cut from £850 to a highly attractive £750. Jensen was contracted to build the bodies from panels made by Boulton & Paul, final assembly being carried out at Longbridge. One change that was made before full production got under way in May 1953 was to raise the headlamps to suit US regulations.

The 100 S models, like the one featured, had a Le Mans package fitted. This included a higher compression ratio, bigger SU carburettors and high-lift camshafts, helping to increase the power from 90 bhp to 110 bhp.

The beautifully kept engine of XNX 770; It has a capacity of 2639cc (161 cu in), turning out 117 bhp. Twin SU HD6 carburettors can be seen on the right and a lead-free head was fitted recently to enable the car to run on lead-free fuel.

A beautifully restored interior is another reason why this is a concours car. Many cars that have been restored can often look better than when they came out of the factory. A well-fitting tonneau hides the two mini rear seats.

Bodies were steel, although the prototypes were aluminium and odd aluminium panels seem to have been used on some early road cars as well as on competition editions. The steel box-section chassis swept under the live rear axle, which was suspended on leaf springs with lever-arm dampers and a Panhard rod, while the front was looked after by coil springs and wishbones with telescopic dampers and an anti-roll bar.

Without doubt a stunning looking car and probably one of the best 3000s around. The owner decided that he wanted something a little more personal and after seeing one in a book that was BMC silver and which had been built for the daughter of Leonard Lord, he decided that was what he wanted. The original car was stripped to the last nut and bolt and then painstakingly rebuilt to the finest of standards.

Speed trials, races and rallies figured with considerable success throughout the life of the Big Healeys, as they were known, and the 100S and later 100M were two special performance editions that came out of this, the former with an all-alloy body, a cross-flow cylinder head, disc brakes and 132 bhp. An extra gear was added in 1955, as was a Morris rear axle, but this factory-coded BN2 was quite short-lived. A new C-series six-cylinder engine of similar capacity had been introduced for the Austin saloons and in 1957 this was fitted to what became the Austin Healey 100/6, distinguished in part by a revised, horizontal-bar grille.

With 102 bhp on tap this was little faster than the 90 bhp 100/4, as it was now known, being longer and heavier, to accommodate two-plus-two seating. Fortunately, it was not long before a new six-port cylinder head lifted power to 117 bhp. Production now transferred from Longbridge to the MG works in Abingdon and soon after a two-seater rejoined the range as an option, albeit on the lengthened chassis.

When the C-series engine was enlarged to 2912cc in 1959, the model became the Austin Healey 3000, now with 124 bhp and a top speed of 183 kph (114 mph). It looked the same as the 100/6, but its transmission was beefed up and it acquired front disc brakes. The 3000 was well reviewed, but in 1961 it was further improved.

A new camshaft and triple SU carburettors (originally twin) upped power to 132 bhp and this MkII was distinguished by a revised grille, once again with vertical bars.

The following summer brought the sophistication of wind-up windows, in place of side-screens, and a new folding hood. Around this time, the two-seater was dropped for good and one of those SUs disappeared again, although power did not suffer.

The final production version of the 3000 was the MkIII. Introduced in 1964, this was the fastest yet, with 148 bhp giving a top speed of 192 kph (120 mph). It was also the most civilised, with a wooden fascia, quarter-lights and, during the run, softer rear suspension with twin radius arms and a modified rear chassis. Although it was getting hard to disguise the big Healey's age, the MkIII undoubtedly gave this timeless beauty a new lease of life. It remained in production until 1967, when forthcoming safety regulations in America, the car's biggest market, were too big a challenge for BMC. Over 72,000 big Healeys were produced – around 14,500 of each of the 100 types and 43,000 3000s.

Before the curtain finally came down, Donald Healey had built a trio of widened MkIIIs with the Rolls-Royce engine from the Vanden Plas 4-litre R and automatic transmission, but this "grand tourer" variant suffered the same fate as its production counterparts and the story was over.

Cars were delivered either with a wood-rimmed steering wheel as shown here, or they might have a plastic version, depending on the specification.

Austin Healey 3000 Mark III 1964

Engine type	In-line six cylinder, ohv
Power	148 bhp @ 5250 rpm
Bore/stroke	83.4 x 88.9 mm (3.28 x 3.5 in)
Capacity	2912cc (177.7 cu in)
Transmission	Rear drive, four gears
Wheelbase	2330 mm (91.7 in)
Top speed	192 kph (120 mph)

This car has been slightly modified. The overdrive standard specification of 22 degrees has been uprated to 28 degrees; whilst the final drive has also been changed from 3.9 to 3.5. As the owner commented: "this makes it very long legged".

Not great if you are touring and you want to put suitcases in the boot, as this is where the spare wheel and battery are stored (right). The engine and engine bay are immaculately clean, even though the car is used regularly (below).

Bentley 3-litre & 4½-litre

As a motor manufacturer in its own right, Bentley was not long lived, but the name conjures up images of speed, style and quality that belie those few years of independence between the wars. Much of the aura comes from a string of successes on the track in the hands of famous drivers, who became known as the Bentley Boys.

When Walter Owen Bentley, always known as WO, set up his own company in Cricklewood, north London, his aim was to build a good, fast car that would be the best in its class. His first product was shown at the Olympia Motor Show of 1919. Known as the 3-litre, this came from the works in chassis-only form, with bodies being supplied by coachbuilders. With a capacity of 2996cc, the engine was advanced for its time, being an in-line four with five crankshaft bearings, aluminium pistons and an overhead camshaft operating four valves per cylinder through rockers.

The 3-litre Bentley was the sports car that put Bentley on the automotive map. Although a larger car than the smaller lightweight Bugattis – which were dominating racing at the time – it was its innovative technology that made up for its weight. Even at 4000 lb (1800 kg), the car won the 24 Hours of Le Mans in 1924 and again in 1927, this time in Super Sports form.

Despite a high price, Bentley struggled to keep up with demand, yet WO found time to produce tuned, lightweight versions of the 3-litre and set up a racing team. Victory in the car's first race, at Brooklands in 1921, showed the way ahead for this little company. Bentleys began to appear on tracks at home and abroad, even Indianapolis having a surprise entry in 1922 from a special which took 13th place against mighty American opposition.

But there is one race with which the Bentley name is synonymous, and that is Le Mans. The first 24-hour race on the French road circuit took place in 1923 and the single Bentley entry took an eventful fourth place, one highlighted inadequacy, stopping power, leading to the introduction of four-wheel brakes for the road cars. Better prepared the following year, the 3-litre won convincingly, with Frank Clement and John Duff at the wheel.

Although luxury saloon bodies were available, it was as a four-seat sports tourer that the 3-litre was famous, the Le Mans bodywork in particular coming from Vanden Plas. A final – and extraordinary – victory at that race for the 3-litre came in 1927, when SCH "Sammy" Davis crashed the famous "Old No 7" at the Sarthe circuit's White House corner but extricated his bent and

The 3-litre car came in many different versions. It was generally delivered as a running chassis with the owner picking what type of body he wanted – many were sent to Vanden Plas for example.

Distinctive radiator and badge. More often than not it was the colour of the radiator badge that distinguished the specification of the car, although this wasn't always the case as the customer could choose whatever colour badge they wanted. This car for example has a red badge, which generally meant that it used a 5.3:1 high compression engine in the 117.5 in (2985 mm) wheelbase chassis and was made from 1924 to 1929.

Bentley 4½-litre 1928

Engine type	In-line four cylinder, overhead camshaft
Power	110 bhp @ 3500 rpm
Bore/stroke	100 x 140 mm (3.94 x 5.51 in)
Capacity	4398cc (268 cu in)
Transmission	Rear drive, four gears
Wheelbase	3300 mm (130 in)
Top speed	151 kph (94 mph)

The engine of this 1928 Bentley 4½-litre had five main bearings, non detachable head and SU Sloper carburettors. Each cylinder also had two spark plugs.

battered mount and went on to take the flag with co-driver Dr Dudley Benjafield.

At this race the 3-litres had been joined by a new 4½. Bentley had introduced a luxury 6½-litre six in 1925 to compete with the likes of Rolls-Royce, Hispano-Suiza and Isotta-Fraschini, but this was never going to be a big-seller and WO was conscious that he needed a replacement for the ageing 3-litre to boost finances. Even so, he was forced to turn to millionaire Bentley owner, Woolf Barnato for a capital injection – which involved Barnato taking over the company and becoming Chairman in 1926.

For the 4½, Bentley reverted to the big four-cylinder engine, to satisfy customers who were missing the "bloody thump" in the smooth six. With bore and stroke dimensions borrowed from the bigger unit, capacity was 4398cc and the engine produced 110 bhp at 3500 rpm, some 30 bhp more than the 3-litre and sufficient for a 151 mph (94 mph) top speed on the road. The stiffened chassis was based on the longer of the two optional 3-litre wheelbases and typical bodywork was very similar.

The 4½-litres came good at Le Mans in 1928, the winning car being driven by Barnato himself, who now confirmed his status as one of the leading "Bentley Boys". Other competition successes were many and sales were good, with 720 4½s built

The large capacity fuel tank was positioned at the rear of the car, making refuelling very easy, once you had figured out how to open the filler cap.

The car had big clear instrumentation, dials that could be read easily by its driver.

Nice touch – but then the whole car was extremely well engineered and thought out. This is the step-up for entering the passenger seats at the rear.

Shown here is the 1928 4½-litre Bentley with a Vanden Plas Touring body. Once the chassis was delivered to the customer, they could then choose from some forty or so coachbuilders to supply a body for them, which would be built to the owner's requirement. Vanden Plas was just one of those coachbuilders.

The water radiator filler cap, matching the one used on the fuel tank, poised neatly on top of the radiator, next to the Bentley badge.

between 1927 and 1930. The 3-litre soldiered on until 1929, by which time 1619 examples had left the works.

Often seen as the classic Cricklewood Bentley, the final 4½-litre variant was not approved by WO. Fitted with Amherst Villiers superchargers by driver Sir Henry "Tim" Birkin and financed by Dorothy Paget, these 50 cars (one of which would be famously driven by Ian Fleming's James Bond) promised great things, with 240 bhp in race trim and 175 bhp for the road, but unreliability foiled the Le Mans victory that Birkin hoped for. The works 6½-litre Speed Six models took those honours in 1929 and 1930, although he gave the Bugattis quite a shock when he finished second in the 1930 French Grand Prix.

By this time, the world was in the clutches of the Great Depression that followed the Wall Street Crash of 1929. Sales slumped and even Barnato's money – or at least his willingness to spend it on keeping the company afloat – was running out. Receivers moved in and Rolls-Royce bought the remnants in 1931. The great days of the sporting Bentleys were gone forever.

BMC Mini

Designer Alec (later Sir Alec) Issigonis was already well known for the Morris Minor when he set out to plan a new baby car for the British Motor Corporation in the mid-1950s. The Suez crisis had brought oil shortages and Issigonis's aim was to provide adequate accommodation for four adults within the smallest practicable exterior dimensions.

Front-wheel drive was not a new idea, but Issigonis applied it ingeniously. Not only did it free up extra interior space by removing the need for a propeller shaft, but in conjunction with the little A-series four-cylinder engine from the Minor, turned round to sit across the car and on top of its gearbox, it helped to make the engine bay astonishingly compact, so that the whole car was only a whisker over 3 metres (10 ft) long.

Prototypes with 948cc engines were deemed by BMC to be faster than was suitable for such a small car, so the stroke was reduced by 5 mm to give an 848cc capacity, with 34bhp being sufficient to power the Mini to just over 113 kph (70 mph). Those prototypes also had the carburettor and exhaust situated at the front, but production engines were reversed, in part to eliminate the issue of carburettor icing (in fact this brought a new problem of distributor flooding in wet weather that beset early cars).

Issigonis's friend Alex Moulton designed rubber spring units that saved further space when combined with wishbones at the front and trailing arms at the rear. Brakes were drums all round, set within tiny 254 mm (10 in) wheels with specially

There had been small cars in the past but the Mini took everybody by surprise. In its original form it had a very long life and even today the new BMW version is as popular as ever. It filled all the requirements of the day – good fuel consumption, space for four, although that could be a little cramped, and it was easy to drive and maintain. It reached all parts of society and many celebrities were happy to be seen not only promoting them but also using them.

Mini 1959	
Engine type	In-line four cylinder, ohv
Power	34 bhp @ 5300 rpm
Bore/stroke	62.9 x 68.3 mm (2.48 x 2.69 in)
Capacity	848cc (51.7 cu in)
Transmission	Front drive, four gears
Wheelbase	2038 mm (80.2 in)
Top speed	116 kph (72 mph)

The Mini was designed as a monocoque shell with welded seams. These are visible on the outside of the car running down the A and C pillars and between the body and the floor pan. To further simplify construction, the car also had external door and boot hinges.

The boot lid was designed with the hinges at the bottom so that the car could be driven with it open, thus increasing luggage space. This design was later discontinued as exhaust gases were found to be leaking into the cockpit while the boot was open. A hinged number plate was also added, so that it could be seen when the lid was down when driving along.

Sliding windows were fitted to the early cars so that the space left on the inside of the doors could be used as storage pockets.

made Dunlop tyres, something that allowed for smaller wheel arches inside of the car.

The combination of the front-wheel drive and a wheel at each corner gave the Mini remarkably good handling, a "nippiness" for which the model soon became renowned. The car was well received by the press, but no one foresaw how this baby would re-shape the motoring world. Announced in August 1959, after only 2½ years in the making it suddenly made other contemporary models seem old fashioned and brought the very word Mini into vogue. It took a while for the rest of the world to catch up, but with few exceptions mini and super-mini cars have had front-wheel drive ever since.

The basic specification was just that, basic, with external hinges, sliding windows, rubber mats, wire-pull interior door openers and only an optional heater. Yet sales quickly built up as the Mini became classless, appealing to young and old alike, as well as to the rich and famous, for whom a suitably

The ADO15, as the Mini was originally designated, used a conventional BMC A-Series, 4-cylinder, water-cooled engine. This was mounted transversely and had the four-speed transmission in the sump. The cooling radiator was mounted at the side and there was front-wheel drive.

The Mini with registration plate 33 EJB, has a grand racing history – in 1963 it took Paddy Hopkirk and Henry Liddon to 3rd overall in the Tour de France, but better was to come. In 1964 the driver and his navigator took first overall in the prestigious Monte Carlo Rally. Paddy Hopkirk and Henry Liddon had achieved a ground breaking victory for Britain and the Mini, fighting off opposition from the Ford Falcon Team and many other very strong competitors. This actual car can be seen at Gaydon Museum of the British Motor Industry in Warwick, England.

customised Mini was a real status symbol. Performance was modest, but with over 64 km (40 miles) possible on a gallon of petrol the economy goal had been achieved.

Famous Formula One manufacturer John Cooper soon saw the performance potential in the car and he went to BMC with his plan for a faster Mini. Managing Director George Harriman gave the go ahead for the programme and the first Mini Cooper, with a twin-carburettor 55 bhp 997cc engine, closer-ratio gears and front disc brakes appeared in 1961 (a bigger-bore, shorter-stroke 998cc unit was substituted in 1964). Built with competition in mind, the Cooper was joined in the pursuit of race and rally success in 1963 by the 1071cc S version, with 70 bhp and servo assistance for the brakes. The following year, to

An original British Motor Corporation (BMC) badge crudely attached to the bonnet of a Mini.

Although Issigonis wasn't keen to see his beloved Mini turned into a performance car, his friend John Cooper, builder of Formula 1 and rally cars, saw the potential of the Mini for competition. The two men collaborated to create the Mini Cooper and so the Austin Mini Cooper and Morris Mini Cooper debuted in 1961. Seen here is a 1964 Morris Cooper Mk I.

Seen here is a 1275cc (77.8 cu in) engine from a Mk III Mini Cooper S of 1972 vintage. Note the twin carburettors and large brake servo.

A temptation to many drivers was to chase a Mini with the big "S" on the boot lid. Featured here is an Austin 970cc (59.1 cu in) "S" version from 1965 – and a very quick little car.

take advantage of 1-litre and 1.3-litre racing classes, the 1071S was replaced by a very short-lived 970S, with 65 bhp, and the 76 bhp 1275S.

Minis of all sorts took competition honours in abundance over the years, but the most famous victories were those of S models in the Monte Carlo Rallies of 1964, 1965 and 1967 (plus 1966, in which a minor headlight infringement brought post-event disqualification).

The Coopers were the first models to replace the long "pudding stirrer" gear lever with a decent remote linkage, which also featured on the up-market Riley Elf and Wolseley Hornet variants introduced with distinctive grilles and vestigial saloon boots in 1962. These were not big sellers, but they remained in production until 1968, as did BMC's attempt at an off-road Mini,

A rare machine is this Innocenti 1300cc (79.3 cu in) Mini Cooper, in right-hand drive. Note the opening quarter light style windows and fitted front wing indicators. The interior of these cars could also look much more comprehensive than their British counterpart.

known as the Mini Moke. This first appeared in 1964, but it had more curiosity value than practical ability, having neither great ground clearance nor four-wheel drive.

The original Minis appeared in Austin Seven and Morris Mini-Minor guises, badging that followed through to the longer estate versions, some with traditional exterior ash framing. Vans and pick-ups were also available as were Deluxe, Super and Super Deluxe trim variations.

In 1964, liquid-coupled Hydrolastic suspension replaced the rubber cones and the transmission and brakes were improved, but the first noticeable change came in 1967, the Mark II Mini having enlarged rear windows, modified grilles and new rear light clusters. A slightly more powerful 998cc engine was now an option, giving a small performance boost and, with a higher final drive, more relaxed cruising. There was even an automatic gearbox option using an ill-fated Automotive Products unit.

Most Mini modifications were made as production changes, but 1969 brought the Mark III models. These had concealed door hinges and wind-up windows, together with the all-synchromesh gearbox and even the heated rear window that had appeared a little earlier. Primarily for cost reasons, the MkIII also reverted to the well-tried rubber suspension.

By now BMC had become the constantly troubled British Leyland and rather than spend money on a replacement for the Mini, the company introduced the Clubman, alongside the standard cars, with a squared-off and extended front and either

By the time that the Mk III Mini had arrived in 1970, there had been some changes. Door hinges were now hidden and there were wind-up windows, by popular public demand.

This is a nicely restored 1970 Mini Mk II, 1275 S from 1970. The door mirror and bonnet catch were not standard but a necessary addition.

the 998cc engine or, for the 1275GT, a detuned version of the Cooper S unit. Saloon versions retained the "wet" suspension for a while, although Clubman estates were "dry" from the start. The Elf, Hornet and Cooper disappeared at this time, although the S soldiered on until 1971.

The old pushrod A-series engine remained throughout the Mini's long life. It was upgraded by varying degrees and it eventually gained single-point – and for the last of a new breed of 1275 Coopers in 1997 – multi-point fuel injection, but it was fundamentally unaltered. Similarly the Mini continued to be updated, for example gaining standard front disc brakes and slightly bigger wheels, but it remained essentially the same much-loved car. Many specialist convertibles were made over the years, but in 1993 an official drop-head entered the catalogue. By the time production, now in the hands of BMW, ended in December 2000, all models had a 1275cc engine.

With 5,387,862 examples produced, the Mini was the best-selling British car ever.

There were many "special editions" of the Mini during the 1980s and 1990s, which gave the car a tag of "fashionable icon". This attracted sales from both home and abroad where people wanted to be seen in a Mini. In Japan it was seen as a "retro-cool icon" and attracted a lot of interest and sales.

A 1991 Mini Mayfair. For many the car had become rather mundane as it complied to new laws governing emissions and safety. There were also newer and more modern cars on the road that also made it look a little dated, but it was still loved by many.

Seen here is the 1750cc (106.8 cu in) engine of the Mini Mayfair. By now all models were fitted with this engine and production was restricted to the Longbridge plant in Birmingham in the West Midlands, England.

Bristol Sixes

Before the Second World War, Bristol was the world's largest aeroplane manufacturer, but during the conflict the directors of the company began to turn their thoughts to building cars. When peace returned, and with the help of H J Aldington, who had imported BMWs in the 1930s, they contrived a delicious cocktail that blended the best features of three of those pre-war models. The chassis of the 326, the looks of the 327 and the engine of the 328 were combined to form the Bristol 400, which was announced in 1947.

What Bristol did then – and has continued to do since – was to apply aircraft engineering standards to car manufacture. Only the best materials and the most painstakingly accurate manufacturing methods were employed to make the 400, which

The Bristol 400 (below) was the first automobile to be built by the Bristol Aeroplane Company (BAC), later to become Bristol Motors. Its body was based on the pre-war BMW 327 and featured a very BMW-like long grille (right). The engine was a slightly modified version of the BMW 326, 6-cylinder pushrod engine of 1971cc (120.3 cu in).

was hailed as a car of remarkable quality and competence, one that was a real pleasure to drive. Nearly every part was made in the factory at Bristol airfield, with its handy 3.2-km (2-mile) long runway/test-strip and invaluable wind tunnel.

The use of that tunnel was evident in the smooth, sleek shape of the two-door, four-seat saloon body. A low, 0.38, drag coefficient coupled with a lightweight steel and aluminium body meant that the 85 bhp 2-litre engine could deliver a top speed of around 158 kph (95 mph). Lovingly assembled and fettled, that engine was a straight-six, with valves inclined in hemispherical combustion chambers and opened via cross-over rockers by a single block-mounted camshaft. Triple carburettors sat atop downdraught inlet ports.

The box-section steel chassis provided sturdy mountings for the suspension. The live rear axle was supported by torsion bar springs and located by an A-bracket, while the independent front set-up used the transverse leaf spring as the lower wishbones. Telescopic dampers were standard, as was rack-and-pinion steering and large drum brakes.

The 401 was quite different from its predecessor, although still using an uprated version of the 2-litre BMW engine. The doors had no handles; a push-button system was inserted into the door and used to open them.

The distinctive bonnet badge of the 2-litre Bristol cars.

The Swiss coachbuilders Beutler, had worked extensively with BMW and so to turn their styling skills to Bristol seemed natural. Seen here is a rare 401 with Beutler bodywork.

The 2-litre, six-cylinder engine of the 401. This was an upgraded version of the 400 unit and benefited from improved Solex carburettors, which boosted the power output.

A luxury model, the 400 was priced accordingly and its discerning owners enjoyed a car that was rewarding to drive but also comfortable over long distances. Its hand-built nature meant that modifications, particularly to power output, could be made to suit individual customers.

The 401 of 1949 put a new, even sleeker body on the 400's mechanical components. Great attention was paid to smoothing airflow, with the rear window, and even the door releases, flush with the skin. A handful of drop-head 402 versions of this car were made for the lucky few.

In 1953, the 403 carried few stylistic changes, but beneath the surface were a 100 bhp engine, a new close-ratio gearbox

and bigger brakes to match. A 1954 modification was the addition of a remote gearchange, which also featured on the distinctive 404 of that year. This was the only production two-seater of the series, with a sweeping coupé tail and vestigial fins that gave a nod to the very special 450 Le Mans racer of 1953 that used large fins for high-speed stability and from 1954 took many class wins.

Power for the 404 was up, with options of 105 or 123 bhp. Dubbed the "businessman's express", this combined its power with lightweight and suitably massive front brakes, mechanical

The Bristol 404 was fitted with a two seat coupé body and introduced in 1953. The rear wings give a real feel for the period. Like the 405, the 404 also moved away from the BMW style radiator grille and utilised a new aero-engine looking front end.

The 403 retained much of the same styling as the 401, although mechanical improvements were made. Bigger valves along with larger main bearings were fitted to the 2-litre engine, which all helped to increase the power output from 85 to 100 hp.

The 406 was the last Bristol to use the BMW-derived, pushrod, six-cylinder engine.This model also featured Dunlop built disc brakes on all four wheels.

arrangements that carried over to the 405 of 1955.

Reverting to the longer wheelbase, the 405 remains the only four-door saloon to have been made by Bristol. Not only did it have an overdrive fifth gear, but like the 404 it had its spare wheel in a compartment behind the left front wheel and its battery and brake servo on the other side to improve weight distribution – something that carries over to today's Bristols.

For the 406, announced in 1958, the engine's bore and stroke dimensions were both enlarged to increase capacity to 2.2 litres. Power was unchanged but torque was slightly up to cope better with increased weight. The 406 was a more conventional three-box saloon than anything before it. It also had disc brakes for the first time, together with a Watt linkage to give more precise rear axle location.

Several of the 400-series models were given alternative bodies by specialist coachbuilders. The best known of these were six lightweight 406 variants commissioned by Bristol from Zagato. These were on standard chassis, but a single car was made on a special short chassis, as was another from Bristol itself. Many other manufacturers have been associated with Bristol – not least AC, which used the six-cylinder engine in the Ace.

As Bristol sought more power, the venerable six finally gave way to an American Chrysler V8 for the 407 of 1961 and a new era began, now under new ownership.

Seen here is the standard 2-litre, 6-cylinder engine of the 405. The drophead version had a highly tuned version of this engine called the 100C, which developed 125 bhp, compared to 105 bhp of the standard 100B engine.

Bristol 405
1956

Engine type	In-line four cylinder, ohv
Power	105 bhp @ 5000 rpm
Bore/stroke	66 x 96 mm (2.6 x 3.78 in)
Capacity	1971cc (120.3 cu in)
Transmission	Rear drive, four gears plus overdrive
Wheelbase	2895 mm (114 in)
Top speed	167 kph (104 mph)

The 405 came in two versions. The more common was the four-door saloon (right), built on the standard chassis of the previous Bristols. The 405 Drophead or 405D (above) had a coupé body by Abbotts of Farnham, England.

The 405 model introduced the ingenious Bristol feature of storing the spare wheel in the front wing (left). Although the only 4-door car ever built by Bristol, the 405 had styling that the company was later to refine for many years on their Chrysler V8-engined cars during the 1960s. The subtle rear wing of the 405 (below), first appeared on the beautifully styled 404

Ford Model Y

As the legendary Model T approached the end of its life, a punitive tax on horsepower ratings in the UK (effectively on bore size) helped sales to slide and the replacement Model A fared little better. After rejecting Henry Ford's proposal for a new light car in 1928, the Chairman of Ford of Britain, Sir Percival Perry, saw that slide accelerate and by 1931 had come to realise that he was wrong. He was forced to plead with Henry to build his new lightweight.

The resulting Model Y, the first Ford to be designed for an overseas market, had probably the shortest gestation period ever. Work began in October 1931 and by the following February 14 prototypes had been constructed in time for the new baby to be shown at the Royal Albert Hall Ford Exhibition of that month.

Henry Ford wanted to bring a new brand name into being for this project, but Perry argued successfully that this would run

The distinctive front view of the "long radiator" Model Y with the starter handle hole through the radiator grille and the dip in the single-groove front bumper. After June 1934, the sidelights and headlights were combined.

The two-door (Tudor) Model Y was named the Ford "Popular" in October 1934 on the introduction of the "De Luxe" Model C. In October 1935, the price of the Tudor was reduced to £100 (120 Euros or US$145 approximately in 2009), the only saloon car ever to be sold at that price. This Model Y is a 1937 Tudor Ford "Popular" in its final design form.

the risk of watering down the potential market and the Ford oval held sway.

The Model Y caused something of a sensation on its launch. It had the hallmarks and the accommodation of a larger car, yet in fully equipped two-door form it went on sale, just a year after Perry wrote his begging letter to Ford, at little over £120, a price that undercut its two home-grown rivals, the Austin Seven and the Morris Minor.

Not surprisingly it was an immediate hit, with 39,000 examples built in 1933, a year in which only 55,000 cars in all left the new Dagenham factory. By the following year, the Y had taken 54 per cent of the market for cars of less than 9 hp.

Technically, the Model Y was somewhat staid. The 933cc engine was a side-valve four, albeit with the then modern refinement of a three- rather than two-bearing crankshaft for added sturdiness and reliability. The rear wheels were driven

through a three-speed gearbox, with the luxury of synchromesh on second and top gears. Both front and rear suspension relied on beam axles with transverse leaf springs, an arrangement that tended to cause the car to wander, and rod-operated brakes were fitted all round.

All cars were four-seaters, but there were options of two or four doors (Tudor or Fordor). A sliding roof was also an option. After the first year or so, the radiator grille was made deeper and the bumper dipped to accommodate this in what is now known as the "long radiator" model. Improvements in production efficiency and simplifications to the body design also enabled

The simple dashboard displayed only an ammeter, a speedometer, an odometer and a fuel gauge. Before April 1935 models had an inserted, engine-turned instrument panel with a hydrostatic fuel gauge.

Ford Model Y
1937

Engine type	In-line four cylinder, side valve
Power	22 bhp @ 3750 rpm
Bore/stroke	56.6 x 92.5 mm (2.23 x 3.64 in)
Capacity	933cc (56.9 cu in)
Transmission	Rear drive, three gears
Wheelbase	2286 mm (90 in)
Top speed	100 kph (62 mph)

The little four-cylinder, sidevalve engine produced 22 bhp at 3750 rpm. With a bore of 2.23 inches (56.6 mm), the fiscal horse-power rating was only 7.956, which rounded up to 8 hp for Vehicle Excise Duty purposes.

Originally, cars were manufactured with only one rear light, located centrally below the bumper. It incorporated a brake light and also illuminated the registration plate. Here we see, also, a spare wheel cover, which was one of the accessories available for the standard model.

Direction indicators are required on vehicles manufactured after January 1 1936. The notoriously unreliable semaphore signals, shown here on this May 1937 car, were the first type to be introduced.

The standard layout of the clutch, brake and accelerator pedals are seen here with the three-speed gearbox gear-stick and the pistol-grip hand-brake lever. The little button seen at the top-left of the picture, is the foot operated dipswitch for the headlights.

As Ford did not produce an open-topped car, to attract punters into their showrooms during the Great Depression, many main Ford dealers commissioned coachbuilders to produce sports cars on the Model Y chassis. Some 30 different designs have been identified.

One of the more attractive convertibles was the "Kerry" sports/tourer, commissioned by W Harold Perry, Ltd., of North Finchley, London, England, and designed and built by Whittingham & Mitchel Ltd., New Kings Road, London, England.

Ford to reduce the price of the two-door model, now called the Popular, to just £100, making it the cheapest four-seat saloon ever in the UK. When the announcement was made at the Ford Exhibition of 1935, the low price quite took the breath away. Competition from the new Morris Eight had been eating into Model Y sales, but this bold move took the market share back up from 22 per cent to nearly double that in 1936.

There was no official convertible – the simple chassis was deemed to be too flexible to cope. The more popular convertibles were commissioned by main Ford dealers to add a bit of glamour to their showrooms during the lean years of the Great Depression. For commercial customers, there was a 5cwt van, which also sold well.

Officially an 8 hp unit, the little engine actually developed 23 bhp, which was sufficient to propel the Model Y to over 97 kph

The dashboard is from the short radiator Model Y, which had black-faced instrumentation. The "Brooklands" fully flexible steering wheel was a standard fitment.

This view of the 8 hp sidevalve engine shows the petrol feed pipe leading from the fuel pump to the Ford/Zenith down-draught carburettor. A cut-out is mounted on the adjustable third brush dynamo.

The attractive four-seater "Kerry" body has "helmet" cycle wings and many "go-faster" superfluous louvres. The body was built on a standard rolling chassis purchased as such from the Ford plant at Dagenham.

(60 mph). Fuel consumption was good, too, with almost 40mpg possible. In both this and later enlarged, 1172cc forms, the side-valve unit continued to drive small Fords way into the 1950s.

Although there was pressure to follow the American trend of changing the design after only two years of production, it was five years before the Model Y was replaced in 1937 by the more streamlined, modern and British-designed Ford 7Y. By then, 157,668 Ys had been built at Dagenham and a total of around 175,000 worldwide.

Ford Lotus Cortina

In its own right, the original Cortina could lay claim to classic status. It set a style on its launch in September 1962 that instantly appealed to the public and soon established Ford as the best-selling UK car manufacturer. There were many variants on that Mark I Cortina (or Consul Cortina, as it was originally badged) theme, but the best was left until last, in the shape of a competition-intended edition engineered by Lotus and known as the Ford Lotus Cortina.

This desirable special was a world away from the sportily badged 1500GT, being conceived for competition and the first of a distinguished line of fast Fords. Walter Hayes was then the new

The classic Lotus Cortina Mk I – its green paintwork and shortened front bumpers make it stand out from all the other Cortina variants. The Lotus Cortina story began around 1961, when the best of Ford and Lotus got together. Colin Chapman had been looking to build his own engines for Lotus for quite some time and his chance came when he commissioned Harry Mundy to design a twin-cam version of the Ford Kent engine.

head of public affairs at Ford in the UK, and he convinced the board that motor sport would do wonders for the brand's image. He knew that Lotus boss Colin Chapman was developing a twin-overhead-cam version of the Cortina's 1500cc engine for use in racing and in the Elan, and so he asked Chapman if he could build 1000 Cortinas thus powered for Group 2 racing (1000 was the minimum to make a model eligible).

Chapman agreed and work began straight away at the Lotus works in Cheshunt. The conversion went far beyond simply dropping in the new power plant. The two-door bodyshell was stiffened and fitted with aluminium doors, bonnet and boot lid.

At the front, the suspension struts were shortened and forged steel lower arms were fitted. The rear leaf springs were replaced by coils, with an A-frame providing axle location, being fixed to the final-drive housing. Light alloy also figured extensively in the transmission casings, while stopping was taken care of by a new Girling brake system, with large front discs sitting within extra-wide wheels and tyres. Weight distribution was improved by moving the battery to the boot.

Chapman had asked Harry Mundy, a noted engineer and Technical Editor of *The Autocar*, to design the aluminium cylinder head. The camshafts were chain driven and operated two valves per cylinder in hemispherical combustion chambers. Fuel was supplied by two twin-choke Weber carburettors (which proved to be a squeeze under the Cortina bonnet).

The result of all the work carried out by Chapman, Keith Duckworth of Cosworth Engineering and Harry Mundy – a stunning twin-cam engine that was the envy of competitors around the world.

Ford Lotus Cortina 1963

Engine type	In-line four-cylinder, ohc
Power	105 bhp @ 5500 rpm
Bore/stroke	82.57 x 72.75 mm (3.25 x 2.86 in)
Capacity	1558cc (95.1cu in)
Transmission	Rear drive, four gears
Wheelbase	2508 mm (98.7 in)
Top speed	174 kph (108 mph)

As with the standard Cortina, the boot area was huge and there was plenty of room for luggage, even with the spare wheel and battery located there.

The Cortina always had pleasing lines. To compensate for the extra weight elsewhere, the car was fitted with an aluminium bonnet, boot lid and doors.

Instrumentation for the Lotus Cortina was increased compared to the standard car and the front seats were also sportier for a better ride at high speed.

Perched in the centre and on the top of the dashboard, on the Mk II version, were the vital engine management dials – left to right: battery condition, oil pressure, water temperature and finally fuel gauge.

The original capacity was the standard 1498cc, but to get closer to the 1600cc class limit, the bores were enlarged, and with 1558cc the twin-cam developed 105 bhp. There was an uprated clutch, while the gearbox casing contained the same close ratios as in the new Elan sports car and a remote linkage was a great improvement on the standard long lever.

Subtle Lotus badging on flanks, boot and grille identified the new model – as did quarter front bumpers and a standard colour scheme of white with a green flash. Inside, there were special seats and instruments, a wood-rimmed steering wheel and a console around the remote change.

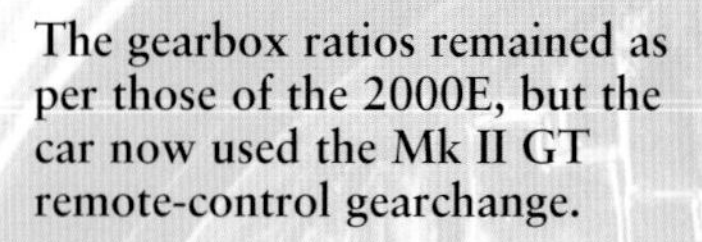

The gearbox ratios remained as per those of the 2000E, but the car now used the Mk II GT remote-control gearchange.

The rear of the new car was a little clumsy, according to many. It didn't have the elegance or the style of the original Lotus Cortina.

The aggressive looking Mk II Lotus Cortina, with the new bodyshell for that model. Ford were by now concerned about the reliability of the Lotus built cars and production was moved to the Ford works at Dagenham and built alongside the GT models. Appearing in 1967, the main difference were the choice of colours and the lack of a stripe, although most customers had them fitted at Ford dealers at an extra cost.

The Lotus input into this new Cortina, launched in January 1963, was evident not just in the name but in the fact that it bore a Lotus type number – 28 – and was built from a Ford bodyshell at the Lotus factory. It was an instant hit, despite initial frailties that so typified Lotus products of the period.

The special rear axle bracing caused oil leaks, so modified leaf spring suspension was fitted to later cars. The gear ratios were changed and the light-alloy casings and panels soon stopped being standard fittings, but the Lotus Cortina was undoubtedly quick. On the track it won the British Saloon Car Championship for Jim Clark in 1964 and went on to take many other wins and series titles. In rallying, success was mixed, but the car's pace was never in doubt and notably won the RAC Rally of 1966 and the Finnish event of the following year.

Production modifications, such as Aeroflow ventilation, mirrored those of the standard Cortina, but in 1966 came the

There were cosmetic changes too, which included a black front grille, 5.5 x 13 inch steel wheels and lotus badges on the rear wings and by the rear number plate. Initially the badge on the front grille was an optional extra.

Along with the dials positioned in the centre of the dashboard, there was still the standard tachometer and speedometer positioned directly in front of the driver.

MkII version of Ford's best-selling saloon and a new Lotus variant joined the range in March the following year. Now built at the Dagenham factory, this was a Cortina Lotus rather than a Lotus Cortina and it had much more in common with its standard stablemates than did the MkI.

Power continued to come from the 1558cc twin-cam, albeit in 110 bhp form, and the transmission and suspension were modified, but in other ways the new car was very similar to the GT. With a wide range of performance options available, the Cortina Lotus remained a serious contender for competition honours, although by now the Twin Cam Escort was taking over.

Although the Lotus engine was used until the end in 1970, the connection went unrecognised from 1969, when Twin Cam badges replaced the Lotus emblems.

Hillman Imp

Hillman's one and only baby car suffered from many frailties, and was a commercial failure that led to Rootes being taken over by Chrysler. Yet the Imp was a much better car than its sales over a 13-year life suggested.

The Rootes Group instructed its designers to come up with ideas for an economical small car in the mid-1950s. This was a market in which the company had no current entrant and the oil shortages that accompanied the Suez crisis of 1956 brought a quadrupling of demand for such cars.

Rear engines were popular in Europe and it was decided that this was the way to go to achieve the goals of compact external dimensions and accommodation for four people. When the Mini took the world by storm in 1959 and set the layout for nearly

Unlike the Mini, its main rival, the Imp had its engine in the rear, whilst the front compartment was the storage area for the spare wheel and any luggage. Although there wasn't a great deal of space it has to be said.

The Hillman Imp was finally launched in 1963 after much development work and several prototypes. Through its prototype stage it was known as "the slug" and later it was reported as the "Ajax". Featured here is a metallic bronze, De Luxe model from 1970.

The sales of 900–1000 cc (55 – 61 cu in) cars quadrupled in the period from 1956 to 1957. The Imp fitted the bill perfectly, with its small shape, small and economical engine, whilst still having a reasonable amount of room inside. Headroom was not a problem once seated, as can be seen – the roof sat quite high compared to the bottom half of the car.

every small car of the future, with a transverse engine and front-wheel drive, the project was too far advanced for changes to be made without starting again.

Fortunately a lightweight engine meant that weight distribution would not be too badly compromised by having the unit behind the rear axle. Specialist builder Coventry Climax developed one of its small racing engines – enlarged from 745 to 875cc and de-tuned to 39 bhp for road use, but still with a light-alloy cylinder block and head and an overhead camshaft. Mounted longitudinally, this drove the rear wheels through a purpose built four-speed transaxle unit with a superb change mechanism.

The rear of the car, where the engine was positioned, was of a simple design. It had the indicator lights and the brake lights positioned one above the other on either side (above), with the engine compartment being easily accessed via two handles and an upward lifting lid (below).

The engine was canted at 45 degrees to fit neatly into the two-door body, which housed the requisite four seats. An opening rear window afforded access to a small luggage space behind the rear seats and there was more room for bags under the front "bonnet", though this was shared with the spare wheel.

Front suspension was by swinging arms, while the rear, also independent, had semi-trailing arms, with coil springs all round. The geometry of the front end meant that wheel camber changes with suspension movement were marked, and until 1967 the static setting was with a distinctly "tucked under" aspect to the wheels. This made the rack-and-pinion steering light and direct and gave the little Hillman remarkably good handling characteristics that belied its tail-heaviness.

Performance was certainly up to the competitive Mini standards of the day, with a top speed of around 121 kph

The rear window of the Imp could be opened, to allow any long items to be fitted inside the car, which created a kind of half hatchback situation. It was also good for extra ventilation on a hot day.

The little 875 cc (53.4 cu in) engine of the Imp, was mounted behind the rear wheels, and slanted at 45-degrees to fit within the rear compartment.

The rather sparse interior of the Hillman Imp never quite matched the Singer variant, but was probably as well equipped and comfortable as its rival, the Mini.

The instrumentation was really quite comprehensive, as can be seen. A selection of necessary dials all neatly placed in front of the driver.

Hillman Imp 1970

Engine type	In-line four-cylinder, ohc
Power	39 bhp @ 5000 rpm
Bore/stroke	68.0 x 60.4 mm (2.68 x 2.38 in)
Capacity	875cc (53.4 cu in)
Transmission	Rear drive, four gears
Wheelbase	2082 mm (82 in)
Top speed	120 kph (75 mph)

There were various models of the Imp. The Singer Chamois was one of the more desirable ones, with its smart paintwork and sporty hatchback style. The speedometer was modern and comprehensive, enclosing both the fuel gauge and water temperature gauge on either side.

The front lights were neatly sunk into the front bodywork. Because of the rather light front-end of the car, the beam often had a tendency to bounce around a little when the little car went over bumps.

(75 mph), and the Imp felt livelier than a 0–100 kph (0–60 mph) time of some 24 seconds implied. Drum brakes all round certainly coped with stopping this lightweight car.

The government lent Rootes a substantial sum to build a new factory for the Imp, but required that this be in a deprived area. Linwood, near Glasgow, was chosen and became a major cause of Imp problems. The car was launched to coincide with the factory's opening in 1963 before it was really ready, and the use of an inexperienced workforce meant that build quality was not what it should have been. The failures and faults that occurred as a result brought a reputation that stuck for the rest of the Imp's life.

A troublesome quirky pneumatic throttle linkage and an automatic choke were two examples of unreadiness. These were soon ditched, but coupled with a persistent cooling unpredictability the sales damage was severe. MkII versions of 1965 incorporated some existing running changes plus slightly better breathing for the engine and improved cooling, while 1968 brought exterior trim modifications and a revised interior. There were also several variants on the theme.

The Singer Chamois (another Rootes product) was a much sleeker looking machine and was seen as an up-market, luxury version of the Imp family. It came in Mark I, Mark II, Sport, & Coupé versions and was equipped with wider wheels and a special front grille.

The Singer Chamois of 1964 had slightly better trim, and the Sunbeam Imp Sport (and Singer Chamois Sport) with twin carburettors and 51 bhp brought a 145 kph (90 mph) top speed two years later. A more sporty style came with the Imp Californian in 1977, also with a Singer version. This had a more steeply raked windscreen and rear window and a lowered roof-line. The Sunbeam Stiletto combined this with the Imp Sport mechanicals later in the year.

The Rallye Imp, produced from 1965 to 1967, was the basis of a very successful competition programme, both for works and private cars. This was sold for homologation purposes and had a 998cc engine, which developed 60 bhp in "standard" form.

There were also van and Husky estate variants, but nothing that Rootes did lifted sales anywhere close to the desired 150,000 a year. Although it struggled on until 1976, Chrysler, which had taken over in 1967, was not interested in updating the car, which was never replaced in the range. Perhaps the Imp was the wrong car for its time, but somewhere there was undoubtedly a very good car looking to be fettled into shape.

The cooling radiator for the Imp was positioned to one side of the engine compartment and had a large cooling fan enclosed in front of it. The little 875 cc (53.4 cu in) engine was really quite economical and could return just under 40 mpg (64 km for every 4.5 litres), something that attracted the buyer during this time of higher fuel prices.

Jaguar XKs

As accidents go, the XK120 was a very happy one. But if it had not been for delays in the production of a new big saloon, the MkVII, the legendary Jaguar XK series might never have existed. Jaguar founder and Managing Director William Lyons (who was to be knighted in 1956) needed a test bed for a new engine and something to exhibit at the 1948 London Motor Show in place of the tardy saloon. He set his team to work to build a sports car around a shortened version of the MkV saloon chassis.

That engine was to become a legend in its own right. A double-overhead-cam straight six with an aluminium cylinder head, it remained fundamentally unaltered as it powered every type of Jaguar for the next 35 years or so. It was originally intended that the unit would be available in four- and six-

Recently fully restored, this is the front-end of a 1950 XK120.

A beautifully kept XK140 Open Two Seater (OTS) from 1955. This is one of only 73 right-hand drive OTS cars and has had little done in the way of restoration. The original owner wrapped all the chassis and under-body in Denso Tape, which has helped to keep the car in its original condition, although the body has seen some repainting over the years.

This XK120 is an original bodied right-hand drive car, one of only 57 made from aluminium and the first XKs off the production line. The wire wheels were fitted when it was modified to compete in hill climb events back in 1953. Originally the car would have had steel wheels and spats.

cylinder forms, but Lyons felt that the prototype fours did not produce enough power and so it was the six, enlarged at the last minute from 3.2 to 3.4 litres for better bottom end urge, that took the stage under the bonnet of the XK120.

The new sports car might have been intended as a "stop gap", but its up-to-the-minute sleek and flowing lines took the public breath away, and demand was immediately such that Lyons knew that this would have to become a production model. The 120 of the name referred to the top speed that could be expected with the new XK engine under the bonnet (X stood for experimental and K was the letter that development units had arrived at, beginning at A, when everyone was happy). A work of art in itself, with its polished cam covers, the engine, with its twin SU carburettors, developed around 160 bhp.

Sitting in the sturdy steel chassis, the straight-six drove a live rear axle through a four-speed gearbox, with synchromesh on the upper three ratios. Front suspension was by wishbones, torsion

Seen from the rear, the XK140 looks sleek and aerodynamic (above). The instrumentation has the usual complement of dials and gauges and is positioned to the left of the driver and in the middle of the dashboard (left). The interior of this car has recently been re-trimmed. Seen here (right) is the straight six, double overhead camshaft engine of the XK140, which can propel the car to a very respectable 224 kph (140 mph).

This 1959, XK150 was originally a left-hand drive car and exported to the USA, spending most of its life in Ohio. Returning to the UK in 1988, it was bought as an abandoned restoration project in 1994. It is hard to believe when seen as it is, but it went through a full rebuild by specialists and converted to right-hand drive. It now participates regularly in long distance tours with The XK Club.

bar springs, telescopic dampers and an anti-roll bar, while the rear axle sat on leaf springs, with lever-arm dampers. Drum brakes figured all round.

The first cars had aluminium bodies, which were exceptionally light, but with demand so high, full production demanded a switch to more easily manufactured steel units and only 244 were in aluminium. That rationed steel was obtained in a deal with the Government that would see a majority of XKs go abroad. In fact, production did not get properly under way until mid-1949 and early cars were all two-seat roadsters with removable windscreens and side screens.

Despite initial scepticism, *The Motor* magazine tested an XK in Belgium at 200.5 kph (124.6 mph), thus justifying the 120 part of the name. Various speed records were achieved by the factory with aerodynamically modified 120s and the car was soon proving itself in competition, especially rallying.

Always quite luxuriously appointed, the roadster was joined in the range by a fixed-head coupé in 1951. This brought real saloon car refinement but combined it with the XK's magical performance, something that continued with the drop-head

coupé of 1953. Rear wheel covers or "spats" were fitted to many examples of all three styles.

After a disappointing *Autocar* fixed-head test in 1951, Jaguar produced two more powerful versions of the XK engine as options. Many of these changes came from the Le Mans-winning XK120C or C-type racer that actually bore very little resemblance mechanically or visually to the road cars.

The same three body variants were available on the XK140 that replaced the 120 in 1954. This had the same chassis, and the same basic shape, but new sturdy bumpers were easy identifiers. Under the skin, rack-and-pinion steering had arrived, together with telescopic rear dampers and a slightly more powerful engine shifted forwards a little to make room for the two occasional rear seats that appeared in the fixed- and drop-head coupés.

After only three years, the final XK, the 150, appeared. Still on the same frame, this had a much more bulky body with a higher

Instrumentation didn't change much from the previous model, although the main dials have been positioned in the middle of the cluster.

The tidy rear-end of the XK150 sees everything in its place – twin rear lights, twin exhaust and twin overrides.

Jaguar XK150
1959

Engine type:	In-line, six-cylinder, dohc
Power:	220 bhp @ 5000 rpm
Bore/Stroke:	87 x 106 mm (3.43 x 4.17 in)
Capacity:	3781cc (230.7cu in)
Transmission:	Rear drive, four gears.
Wheelbase:	2951mm (102 in)
Top speed:	224 kph (140 mph)

The beautifully restored straight-six engine of the XK150, which is fed by Twin 1.75 inch (44.5 mm) SU carburettors.

waist-line, but it had also gained all-round disc brakes for the first time. A new cylinder head with three carburettors gave customers the option of an extra 20 bhp or so, an option that continued in an S variant when the XK engine's capacity was enlarged to 3.8 litres. Increased weight and frontal area had eaten into the XK's performance, but the 150S was nonetheless a fast car, as well as a very comfortable one, with a top speed of 212 kph (132 mph).

When production ended in 1961, a shade over 30,000 XKs had been built. Not bad for a stop gap!

Jaguar E-type

If the XK series took Jaguar into competition, it was the E-type that resulted directly from those hugely successful race track forays. Launched in 1961 to an astonished press and public reaction, this magnificent sports car was a direct descendant of the D-type racers that had dominated the Le Mans 24-hour race in the 1950s.

Having achieved such success in that event, Jaguar boss Sir William Lyons decided to withdraw the works team from competition (the all-conquering 1957 D-types were private entries) and concentrate on a new road-going sports car. The XKs were still in production, but the C-types and D-types that had grown out of them were very different from them.

Whichever way you see it, the Jaguar E-type, or XK-E as it was known in the US, is without doubt one of the sexiest cars ever designed. When launched it caused a sensation and even today it turns heads and creates attention to its stunning lines and powerful engine. Featured here is a beautifully restored 1961, Series I, 3.8-litre roadster and is typical of the early cars that came off the production line.

Work started in 1957 on the new car, and a number of prototypes were built to achieve Lyons's aim of building a sports car that adopted the best parts of the racers and adapted them for fast but genuinely comfortable road use. Power was to come from the XK straight-six that had already proved itself both in the road cars and on the track. The original intention was for this twin-overhead-camshaft unit to have a capacity of around 3 litres, and a power output of some 285 bhp, but in the event it was the longer-stroke 3.8-litre unit from the XK150S, with 265 bhp that went into the production cars.

No real sports car of the 1960s would be without a wooden steering wheel. The 3.8-litre cars have leather-upholstered bucket seats, an aluminium-trimmed centre instrument panel and console and a 4-speed gearbox without synchromesh in first gear – generally known as a "Moss box".

The Series I can easily be identified as it has its indicator and tail-lights positioned above the bumpers (left) and the exhaust tailpipes under the registration plate at the rear of the car (below).

Unlike previous Jaguars, whose styling had been finalised by Sir William himself looking at mock-ups and having modifications made to suit his expert eye, the E-type was the work of aerodynamics expert Malcolm Sayer, who had been responsible for the D-type and its limited edition road-going offspring the XKSS.

Hailed by many as the most beautiful car of all time, his creation was right in all its proportions. Its seductive curves flowed and it simply had the air of a car that would be an exceptional performer. Announced at the 1961 Geneva Motor Show, the E-type caused a sensation: it was headline news both in the motoring press and in the national dailies. Not only did it have looks to die for but it was unbelievably inexpensive. At just over £2000, it was under half the price of its nearest rivals, the Ferrari 250GT and the Aston Martin DB4.

Not only did it borrow its style from the D-type but it was similar in its construction. Unlike the XKs, the E-type had no separate chassis. A steel monocoque tub extended from the front bulkhead to the rear of the boot and a tubular front framework

Just visible through the slats on the bonnet is one of the three SU carburettors that feed the 3.8-litre powerplant.

All E-types featured four-wheel disc brakes and all were power-assisted. Jaguar was one of the first car manufacturers to equip their cars with disc brakes as standard from the XK150 model in 1958. Optional extras included chrome-spoked wheels and a detachable hard top for the roadster.

was bolted to this to carry the engine, the front suspension and steering, and the one piece "bonnet" that hinged forward. The Moss gearbox was nothing to be proud of. With a ponderous long-throw change and no synchromesh on first, the four-speed unit left a lot to be desired.

A major difference from the D-type was the fitting of independent rear suspension, also on a subframe that could be removed easily for maintenance. The drive shafts were used as the upper of a pair of transverse links with a lower radius arm, and there were twin coil springs and telescopic dampers each side. At the front, there were torsion bars, double wishbones and an anti-roll bar. The powerful brakes were discs all round, mounted inboard at the rear, for low unsprung weight. With centre-lock chrome wire wheels this new Jaguar really did look the part.

The two-seater came in roadster and coupé body styles, both with well-appointed interiors that lacked the polished walnut of the saloons but retained the

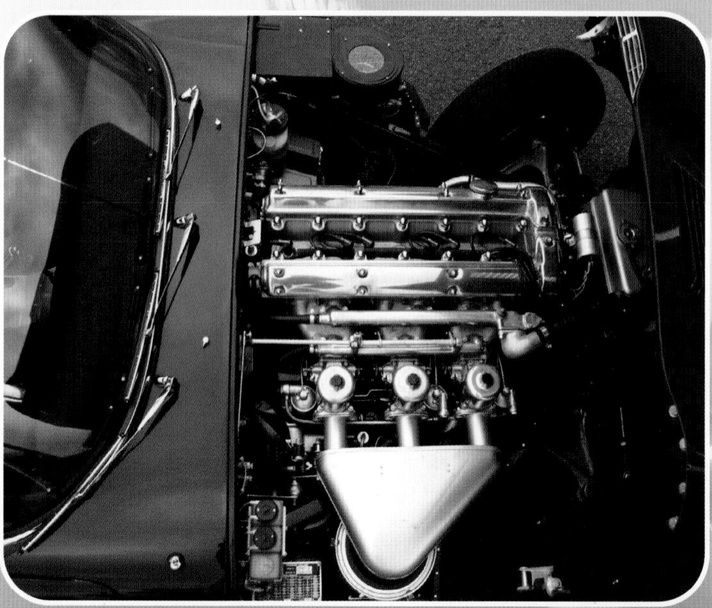

A great view of the 3.8-litre engine inherited by the Series I, E-type and which was fitted to the legendary XK series. This engine along with the aerodynamic shape of the E-type produced incredible performance figures for the time.

Instrumentation was very comprehensive – there was plenty going on to keep the driver occupied. The switches shown were one of the changes made for the intermediate cars, which had to comply with US safety regulations.

Jaguar E-type
1961

Engine type	In-line six-cylinder, ohc
Power	265 bhp @ 5500 rpm
Bore/stroke	87 x 106mm (3.43 x 4.17 in)
Capacity	3781cc (230.7cu in)
Transmission	Rear drive, four gears
Wheelbase	2438 mm (96 in)
Top speed	241 kph (150 mph)

The Series I can also be recognised by the glass covered headlights (above), at least up to 1967 when US legislation dictated that they had to be open style. The small "mouth" opening at the front of the car was also a give-away (right).

host of dials and switches. The aerodynamic effect was rounded off by flush transparent covers over the inset headlamps.

The E-type was a fast car by any standards, with handling well up to scratch on a choice of Dunlop road or racing cross-ply tyres. The 241 kph (150 mph) top speed obtained by leading magazines in their tests was, it later turned out, thanks to some special treatment given by the factory to the press car. Nobody minded. This Jaguar remained a 241-kph car in the eyes of most enthusiasts.

From the start, the E-type was every bit the practical road car, with no official competition programme. However, in private

The aluminium-trimmed centre instrument panel and console was changed to vinyl and leather in 1963, although instrumentation remained similar and comprehensive.

The 4.2-litre cars were fitted with more comfortable seats, improved brakes and electrical systems and an all-synchromesh four-speed gearbox. An easy way to identify one is to look for a badge on the boot proclaiming "E-type Jaguar 4.2".

hands it saw quite a bit of racing success. The first few right-hand-drive cars went to racing customers and wins came immediately, not least in the hands of Graham Hill. The factory had the best of both worlds. It could reap the commercial benefits of racing glory without the associated costs.

To this end, a dozen lightweight E-types were created between 1962 and 1964 for individual customers. These had aluminium panels supported on special steel framing, plus an integral aluminium hard-top. The lightest of all had an aluminium-alloy cylinder block (the head was already aluminium), although this was too susceptible to distortion if overheated for endurance racing reliability.

The first significant change to the road cars came in 1964, when the XK engine was enlarged to 4.2-litres by increasing the bore size. At the same time, Jaguar finally produced its own all-synchromesh gearbox, with a relatively slick change, coupled to an uprated clutch. The interior was made more plush and the machined aluminium instrument panel was replaced by a black finish.

Around 75 per cent of E-type production went to the USA and it was with that market in mind that the 2+2 was introduced in 1966. The wheelbase and body were lengthened and the coupé's roof was raised to squeeze two small rear seats into what had been luggage space in front of the side-opening rear window. There was no convertible version, but the 2+2 could be had with automatic transmission for the first time.

By now, the headlamp covers had gone and there were one or two other minor changes in what became unofficially known as the Series I½. More significant were the alterations that came with the Series II in 1968. This had new brakes and could be ordered with power steering, while the exterior was easily distinguished by an enlarged air intake in the bonnet and raised bumpers with new front and rear lamp clusters below. The distinctive three-wiper arrangement for the now more inclined windscreen had also gone. Inside, rocker switches had replaced the toggles of earlier cars.

By now Jaguar was developing its new 5.3-litre V12 engine, destined for the XJ-S, but delays to that car brought in the Series III E-type in 1971. Although officially still available with the

Not too much had changed as far as instrumentation was concerned, although the switches had now become the "rocker" type, as defined by US legislation.

Aggressive exhaust pipes and a very obvious badge on the rear door, show instantly that this is a Series III, V-12 E-type. Whitewall tyres were mainly seen in the US, although they weren't unfamiliar in the UK also.

In Series III form, the E-type was restricted to being a convertible or a 2+2. The latter also had an opening back door and a reasonable storage area, for a sports car anyway!

straight-six, all but one S3 sold had the V12. With one overhead camshaft per bank, this produced a genuine 272 bhp, although the now much heavier car was probably slightly slower than the original 3.8.

All Series IIIs (there was no two-seat coupé) were on the long wheelbase and they looked very different from the originals, with flared wheel arches and wide wheels and tyres, along with an altogether more dumpy appearance. Manual and automatic transmissions were available on both types while the suspension geometry was altered and ventilated front discs added to cope with the extra weight.

The 2+2 was dropped in 1973, but the roaster soldiered on into 1975, by which time more than 72,500 E-types had been built.

A new V12 engine was introduced for the Series III cars, which had a capacity of 5343cc (326 cu in) and was fed by four Stromberg carburettors. With 246 bhp at its disposal, the car could reach a maximum speed of 234 kph (146 mph) but only returned a miserly 14 mpg (23 km for every 4.5 litres) under everyday driving conditions.

The front grille was now a large chrome trimmed intake and the road wheels were considerably larger than before, giving the car a very aggressive appearance.

Jensen Interceptor

If the Jensen brothers, Alan and Richard, had had their way, the Interceptor would never have existed. In the mid-1960s, they wanted to build a sports convertible, called the P66 in prototype form. This was to supplement the up-market C-V8 in the range and fill a gap in the American market that they guessed would be left by the forthcoming demise of the Austin Healey 3000, for which Jensen built bodies. One prototype was exhibited at the 1965 Earls Court Motor Show, but production never got under way, the brothers being outvoted by a majority of the Jensen board, which wanted to concentrate on devising a replacement for the C-V8.

The biggest bone of contention was the decision to solicit the services of an Italian styling house to come up with a design and

The interior of Jensen cars was always plush and glamorous – no exception to the inside of this 1968 model.

Seen here is a beautiful example of an early Mk I Interceptor. They were made between 1966 and 1969, before the Mk II was introduced in 1970. Although a heavy car the big Chrysler V8 engine had no problems pulling it along. From a standing start to 96 kph (60 mph) could be achieved in 7.3 seconds, which is quite something for a car this big.

the episode, piled on top of ill health, led to the retirement of Alan and Richard. Ghia, Touring and Vignale were asked to submit their ideas and it was one from Touring that was adopted, although that company's parlous state meant that the design was bought outright and passed to Vignale to develop the car for production.

The Interceptor name had been used on two earlier models and it was revived for this C-V8 replacement, which was introduced to the public at the 1966 London Show. Although it was based on the earlier car's tubular chassis and shared its wheelbase and track dimensions, the frame was now welded to steel bodywork, rather than clothed in glassfibre. Whatever the Jensen brothers believed, the new fastback saloon shape was undoubtedly elegant, with two doors and four seats.

Power was provided by the same Chrysler engine as in the C-V8. This 6.3-litre V8 came with pushrod-operated overhead valves and a single Carter four-barrel carburettor. The gross power output was 325 bhp at a modest 4600 rpm, with a massive 425 lb ft of torque at only 2800 rpm. The engine came with a Chrysler Torqueflite three-speed automatic transmission. A four-speed manual gearbox was an option but only a handful of cars were ever thus equipped. Top speed was over 209 kph (130mph).

Jensen Interceptor
1968

Engine type	V8, ohv
Power	330 bhp @ 4600 rpm
Bore/stroke	107.95 x 85.73 mm (4.25 x 3.38 in)
Capacity	6276cc (383.6 cu in)
Transmission	Rear drive, three-speed automatic transmission
Wheelbase	2667 mm (105 in)
Top speed	219 kph (137 mph)

The big car was ideal for touring and a neat up-lifting, large rear window gave good access to a spacey rear boot area, perfect for any luggage.

This was no small vehicle, at 15-ft 8-ins (4.8 m) it stood its ground and could be a little intimidating. Production totalled at 1024 for the Mk I, which included 78 left-hand drive models.

The gorgeous leather interior was sumptuous and comfortable, although the passengers didn't have too much leg room, even though the car was long and sleek.

One side of the big Chrysler V8, D-series engine, which was attached to a Chrysler Torqueflite, 3-speed automatic gearbox. Only 24, 4-speed manual variants were made in the Mk I version.

Although the Mk II Interceptor looked very similar to the earlier Mk I, there were quite a few changes, some subtle, others not so subtle. The exterior had cosmetic changes but the basic shape remained.

The dashboard of the Mk II certainly changed, with the instruments being spaced out rather than restricted to a central panel. Switches were now the "rocker" type also.

Double wishbones, coil springs and telescopic dampers looked after the front suspension, while the rear relied on a simple live axle, with leaf springs and a Panhard rod, again with telescopic dampers, and now time-driver adjustable. Steel wheels were shod with cross-ply tyres for the first few years and disc brakes were fitted all round.

The Interceptor was a luxury car, and was suitably furnished, with leather seats and trim and deep Wilton carpets. The price reflected this and the Jensen's hand-built nature: £3700 sounds very little now, but a launch price of £1797 for the 4.2-litre Jaguar XJ6 in 1968 puts this in perspective.

Jensen quickly realised that having bodies made in Italy did not make economic or practical sense, so manufacture was shifted to the factory. Quality quickly improved as a result.

To the untrained eye, the car that sat alongside the Interceptor at Earls Court in 1966 was a duplicate. In fact this had a 76 mm (3 in) longer front end, the length added to accommodate the Ferguson four-wheel drive system. This was the FF, which also had Dunlop Maxaret anti-lock braking. Crude and scary by today's standards, this gave the FF additional caché in this prestige market. Despite considerable extra weight, the FF was not too much slower than the Interceptor and its rear-biased four-wheel drive gave it additional surefootedness. Unfortunately it was very expensive to build and even with a 42 per cent higher price tag its greatest value to the company was in the excellent publicity that it generated for the Interceptor.

Minor changes were made to both types in the course of production, including the misguided introduction of a Director edition in 1969, with built-in office equipment of the day. A proper Mark II Interceptor appeared in 1970, with minor styling differences and alterations to the suspension, not least the removal of adjustable dampers. Inside, the fascia was substantially revised. This was followed a year later by the Mark III, with wider wheels and ventilated discs, and the SP. SP was short for Six Pack, denoting the six intakes for the three twin-choke carburettors that were fitted to the new 7.2-litre V8. At 230 kph (143 mph), this was the fastest Interceptor, but its carburettors were set up so that some throttles were operated by vacuum from the inlet manifolds and this caused sudden unnerving surges of power.

The FF was dropped in 1971 and the Mk III gained a detuned and stable 7.2-litre engine in 1973, when the SP disappeared again. In the following year, a stylish four-seat convertible, spoiled only by the raised bulk of the stowed hood, and a coupé – a sort of hard-top version of the drop-head – joined the range.

Jensen went into receivership in 1976 and production ended. Jensen Parts & Service became Jensen Cars Ltd and re-introduced the Interceptor in Mk IV form in 1983, with minor modifications and a new 5.9-litre V8. However, very few cars were made between then and 1993 when, in new hands once more, production finished for good, with nearly 6000 cars built.

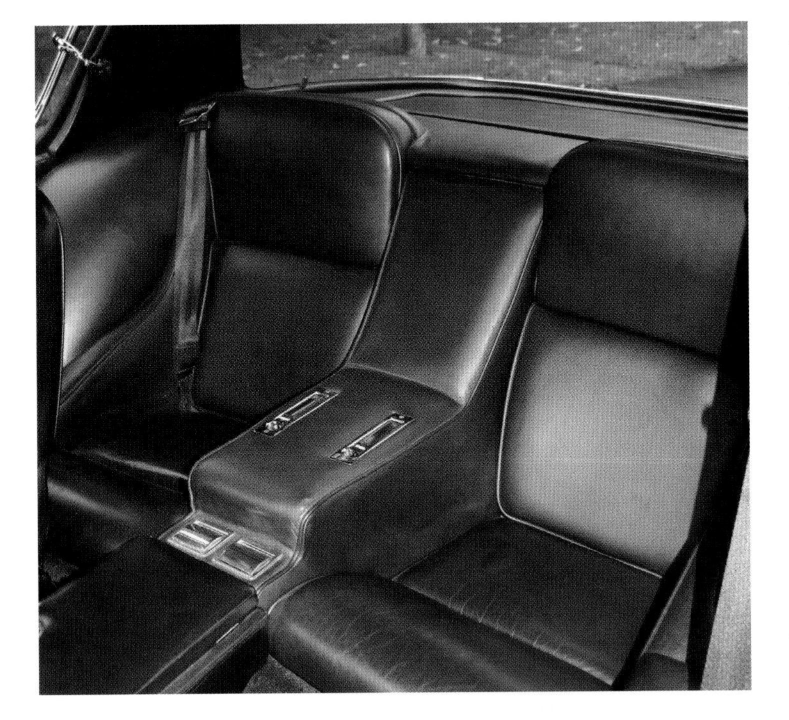

The rear accommodation of the Mk II, although similar to the Mk I, was in fact quite different and had a much deeper seat with more pronounced central section.

The front-end of the Interceptor II changed little from its predecessor.

A big engine needs plenty of cooling. The Mk II version still used the Chrysler engine, the V8 J series. Capacity was up but power output went down as did top speed.

Lagonda 4½ Litre

In the 1930s, Lagonda got itself into trouble, largely through simultaneously offering a profusion of different models, some with the company's own engines and others with proprietary units. Such was the dire situation that the business was pronounced bankrupt in 1935, although it was quickly purchased from the receivers by young solicitor Alan Good.

Ironically, a Lagonda won the Le Mans 24-hour race during the receivership and it was the racing prowess of the winning 4½-litre model that was instrumental in snatching the company from oblivion. Not only did the victory bring investment, but it also brought W O Bentley, recently released from Rolls-Royce duties, on board as Technical Director.

Lagonda was new to the "bought-in" components side of the business, but 1933 saw them install a 4.5-litre, Meadows, 6-cylinder engine into a modified 3-litre chassis, which resulted in the M45 model. Seen here is the very stately ST34, saloon version of 1934.

The 4½-litre itself came out of a proposition from a group of racing drivers that the company should put such an engine into a 3-litre chassis. Although the deal that was struck fell through, the development work continued and the new car was introduced in late 1933 as the M45. Sturdy chassis members were diagonally braced and carried solid axles at both ends on semi-elliptic leaf springs, with friction dampers. The four-wheel drum brakes were mechanically operated. Power came from a Meadows straight-six, also used by Invicta until its 1933 collapse.

This was an iron pushrod overhead-valve unit with four main bearings and it managed to combine low weight with a prodigious low-speed torque output. Lagonda avoided quoting a power figure, but did suggest 108 bhp on one occasion when pressed. At first, the company's own gearbox was used, but this was later ousted in favour of the Meadows variety.

Lagonda 4½ litre 1934

Engine type	In-line six cylinder, ohv
Power	108 bhp @ 3100 rpm
Bore/stroke	88.5 x 120.6 mm (3.48 x 4.75 in)
Capacity	4453cc (271.7 cu in)
Transmission	Rear drive, four gears
Wheelbase	3124 mm (123 in)
Top speed	152 kph (95 mph)

A 50-percent increase in power was obtained with no increase in weight, which produced dramatic performance gains and another instant success for the factory. Such was the demand for the new M45 that the factory had some difficulty keeping up with supply.

The powerful Meadows engine had no trouble pulling the lightweight 3-litre body of the M45. The second of the two SU carburettors is just visible in this picture.

The driver was spoilt with instrumentation, which was scattered all over the dashboard of this M45.

Lagonda built many of its own bodies at its works in Staines, near London, but specialist coachbuilders were also employed. Open tourer styles were the most common, with two or four seats, but there were also four-door saloons. The principal opposition came from the considerably more expensive Bentley 3½ litre, which could just pip the M45's 153 kph (95 mph) top speed.

An M45R or Rapide version was announced in 1934. This shared modifications with successful racers of that year, such as a shorter wheelbase, new Girling brakes and an uprated engine. It also had a fashionable freewheel device behind the gearbox.

And so it was that a Lagonda crossed the Le Mans finishing line first in 1935, but nothing changed the mess that the company was in and new boss Good decided that there should

Tucked away by the right leg of the driver (on this right-hand drive car) was the handbrake and gearchange lever – both beautifully finished and surrounded at the bottom by leather skirts.

Lagonda, unlike Bentley who didn't supply their own bodies at the time, were able to offer their customers a range of factory-built bodies. There was a choice which included both open and closed types, but without doubt the most handsome was the tourer (above and left). This has a factory "T7" body fitted but there were also other bespoke coachbuilders such as Vanden Plas, Wylder, and Freestone & Webb who also were happy to supply bodies for the M45.

be but one model, the 4½ litre, and that this should be the best car in the world. Bentley's first pressing task was to refine the car and those initial efforts resulted in the LG45, which was launched in September 1935. Mechanically, it was a slightly detuned Rapide, but it was quieter inside and out, had synchromesh on third and top gears and hydraulic dampers for the first time. New, more curvaceous body styles were also available.

The Rapide name quickly reappeared on the LG45. This was a glamorous, flowing, open four-seater, with "helmet" wings and a rounded tapering tail. The standard LG could already manage 160 kph (100 mph), but the Rapide, with further engine work, could move on to 174 kph (108 mph). Thanks to the earlier

The Meadows engines had a reputation of being robust and the 4½ litre was no exception. When the M45 was launched it was the largest-engined British sports car available and because it was such a well-engineered unit, it was ideal for tuning and racing.

toughening of the bottom end, W O had been able to take the engine through three Meadows-sanctioned performance increases (thus Sanctions 1, 2 and 3), the last of which had a Weslake cylinder head.

The Rapide did not have room for the Bentley's new gearbox – with synchromesh on the upper three ratios and a central gear lever – that was by now fitted to standard cars, but for 1937 came a new chassis, in three lengths, with independent front suspension by double wishbones and torsion bars. With the Sanction 3 engine, this was known as the LG6, but this splendid new car was really made to accommodate Bentley's new masterpiece, a 4½-litre V12.

An especially light and tough unit, this had overhead camshafts and produced less torque but more power than the straight-six. Two stripped and modified V12s, with over 200 bhp, were raced steadily to third and fourth places at Le Mans in 1939 in preparation for an all-out assault the following year. Alas, war put paid to the race and, ultimately to the 4½ litre and its V12 engine.

In September of 1936, Lagonda announced the LG45 Rapide as "the fastest car in the world". It used the engineering found on the LG45R racing cars but was dressed in a stylish touring body. Styling came from Frank Feeley and the car featured four seats, cutaway doors and American-style, chrome exhaust pipes that snaked their way out from the side of the bonnet.

Many of the controls could be found on the steering wheel but dials were large and clear (below). The rear of the car was quite well enclosed, with even the exhaust pipes being surrounded by bodywork (right).

Land-Rover

At the end of the Second World War, the British government rationed steel. Yet Rover was anxious to come up with a new model to make use of its huge Solihull factory that was no longer making aero engines.

The steel shortage ruled out most ideas for the time being, but then Chief Designer Maurice Wilks was looking for a replacement for the Jeep he used on his farm in Anglesey. He and his brother, Managing Director Spencer Wilks, set about designing their own vehicle, something that would do all that the Jeep could do and plenty more.

Steel was required for the chassis, which was welded into box sections from flat strips in what became a Land-Rover tradition,

Originally designed for farm and light industrial use, the first prototype was built in the summer of 1947. This was followed by a further 48 examples that were built for trials and appraisal. The Land-Rover was launched in April 1948 at the Amsterdam motor show and was originally designed as a short term project to keep the Rover car company busy until the depressed post-war car market started to pick up.

The Series I had a box-section steel chassis and aluminium bodywork. This was due to the rationing of steel and the abundance of aircraft aluminium. There are still many examples on the road today, restored and not restored. The one featured here can be seen at the Heritage Motor Museum at Gaydon, England.

Land-Rover
1948

Engine type	In-line four cylinder, overhead inlet, side exhaust valves
Power	55 bhp @ 4000 rpm
Bore/stroke	69.5 x 105 mm (2.74 x 4.13 in)
Capacity	1595cc (97. 3 cu in)
Transmission	Four-wheel drive, four gears
Wheelbase	2032 mm (80 in)
Top speed	80 kph (50 mph)

The interior of the 1948 Land-Rover is basic, for example there is only one windscreen wiper. The passenger side wiper was an extra. The transmission tunnel was an angular construction and bolted to the firewall and had the gear lever protruding through it. The red topped lever was for engaging hi/low ratio gears.

but for the bodywork, aluminium alloy provided the answer. Relatively abundant now that it was not needed for aircraft production, this was also attractive because it was easy to hand work and would not rust, a useful feature on a vehicle that might spend much of its life getting very wet and muddy.

Early prototypes had a central steering position and were powered by a 1.4-litre Rover 10 petrol engine, but when the new Land-Rover reached production in 1948 it was fitted with a 50 bhp 1.6-litre four from the equally new Rover 60.

Permanent four-wheel drive was a feature and in order to prevent tyre scrub on the road, a lockable freewheel was fitted between front and rear axles. Leaf springs looked after suspension and gave good ground clearance, while drum brakes were fitted all round. Designed from the start as a work horse, the Land-Rover had a power take-off to drive farm equipment. There was just an open-topped body to start with and this made no concessions to comfort – just basic seats and no niceties such as trim or a heater.

It was soon clear that this was going to be much more than a stop-gap. Sales took off, helped by the fact that the Land-Rover avoided the purchase tax that was then applied to private cars. The same was

The 1948 Land-Rover used a 1.6 litre, 4-cylinder Rover engine from the P3 road car range. The engine was upgraded to 2-litres for 1952 and two years later the Land-Rover was given a complete upgrade.

Not the biggest or most visible speedometer, but other essential gauges and switches were positioned alongside in the centre of the dashboard.

Trafficators were not standard equipment and classed as an added extra. They could be ordered with the vehicle or even added afterwards.

not true of the short-lived station wagon that came in 1949, with Tickford wood-framed coachwork, seven seats and relative luxury.

The Land-Rover was quick to prove itself a highly capable off-road vehicle. It could cope with rough terrain, steep hills and rutted, muddy conditions. Armed forces, both in the UK and overseas, soon took up the new vehicle for their own use and over the ensuing half-century there have been innumerable military versions, with such features as caterpillar tracks, forward control, armour plating and removable panels.

The freewheel soon disappeared in favour of a selectable two- or four-wheel-drive system, with high and low sets of gear ratios. Power increased, too, with the coming of a 2-litre engine. Other early changes included the headlamps moving forward from behind the grille. The wheelbase was extended by 152 mm (6 in) in 1953 (to 2184 mm) to silence complaints about lack of load space, and there was now also a long-wheelbase 2718 mm (107 in) version option for those who still felt cramped.

Strangely, the factory-built station wagon, of 1954, was on the short chassis, but the following year brought the first long-wheelbase estate, with seating for up to 10 people. Five doors could also be had for the first time.

The forthcoming introduction of a diesel option necessitated another 51 mm (2 in) being added to the wheelbase in 1956. With overhead valves (the petrol unit still had side exhausts), what was one of the new breed of high-speed diesels developed 50 bhp from its 2 litres.

A major update came with the Series II models of 1958. Styling looked much the same, but a few curved edges had been

Wacky or what! This is the Land-Rover Cuthbertson tracked vehicle, which has demountable tracks fitted to it. This example is fitted to an 88-inch 24V FFR, Series I Land-Rover, but there are also other Cuthbertson conversions. It is thought that 15 units were made by Cuthbertson of Biggar, Scotland, the last being built in 1972.

During the Series III production run from 1971 until 1985, the 1,000,000th Land-Rover rolled off the production line in 1976. Featured here is that vehicle, which can be viewed at the Heritage Motor Museum, Gaydon, England.

The Series III saw many changes in the later part of its life as Land-Rover updated the design to meet increased competition. This was the first model to feature synchromesh on all four gears.

The Series III is the most common Series vehicle, with 440,000 of the type built from 1971 to 1985.

added to the slab-sided bodies. After a while, a new 2.25-litre petrol engine, based on the diesel, was introduced, as was synchromesh on third and fourth gears. In 1961, the diesel was enlarged to match and this pair continued to power Land-Rovers for the next 20 years or so.

The description of the station wagon that appeared in 1962 as a 12-seater was probably stretching a point, but it allowed this variant to be registered as a bus and thus to avoid purchase tax. This advantage put paid to the old 10-seater that was still on the 2718 mm (107 in) wheelbase.

Six-cylinder petrol power was offered for the first time, on the long wheelbase, in 1966, with a 2.6-litre engine from the Rover saloons. This was primarily intended for the heavy forward-

The headlights were moved to the wings on late production IIA models from 1968/9 onward, to comply with Australian, American and Dutch lighting regulations and remained in this position for the Series III.

The traditional metal grille, featured on the Series I, II and IIA, was replaced with a plastic one for the Series III model.

There was plenty of seating space in the rear of the vehicle and access was easy via the large rear door.

control versions, but a heavy-duty One Ton model was announced in 1968, with many of that type's uprated components and systems. The headlamps finally found their way to the wings the following year.

A Series III edition was launched in 1971 by what was now British Leyland. This looked much the same, but its interior had been freshened up, with a new instrument panel and an efficient heater. Engines were little changed, but a new gearbox had synchromesh on all forward speeds and the ratios for both the high and low sets were altered.

As the 1980s dawned, the strength of various components was upgraded, not least with five-bearing crankshafts for the four-cylinder engines. The company sought a new leisure market with the rather softer County models of 1982 – these even had soundproofing! A pick-up had long been an option, but a long-wheelbase type now appeared.

The biggest change of the 1970s was the fitting of the Range Rover's 3.5-litre V8 as the decade drew to a close. These long-wheelbase Land-Rovers had permanent four-wheel drive, but could still only manage around 129 kph (80 mph) on the road.

What by Land-Rover standards was a major redesign came in 1983. Wheelbases were lengthened again for the 110 and the 90 of the following year. Wider track was covered by wheel arch extensions and the V8 was a standard option, along with slightly enlarged, 2.5-litre petrol engines and full-time four-wheel drive. Most importantly, coil springs replaced the old leaves, giving better ride quality and, for the worst surfaces, longer wheel travel.

The choice of aluminium for the body panels goes back to the original Land-Rover of 1948, a time when sheet steel was in short supply. Thus Rover decided to build their new car with aluminium bodywork. It is interesting to know that the 2008 Defender models still use aluminium body panels.

The "aluminium" Land-Rover Series III was produced as a show model and is distinctive for its polished aluminium body and a transparent bonnet, which was designed to reveal the structure of the car.

There was a move to give more comfort with interior furnishings with the Series III cars and the instrumentation was now also repositioned in front of the driver rather than being centrally mounted on the facia.

County models became ever better equipped and still-longer wheelbases appeared, as, in 1986, did a 2.5-litre turbo-diesel. By now Land-Rovers were facing fierce competition from rivals, especially in export markets, and the new engine was intended as a quick fix to improve performance.

The latest incarnation of this old work horse hit the showrooms in 1990, the Defender badge distinguishing this from the Discovery and, more recently, the Freelander. An updated turbo-diesel rendered other engine options obsolete until it too was replaced in 1998 by a five-cylinder turbo unit in the Td5. Many changes have continued to be made to appeal to the leisure market, including the addition of air conditioning and heated seats to the options list.

The Series III vehicles were introduced in 1971 and were mechanically similar to the Series IIA but featured a new all-synchromesh gearbox.

The 2008 Defender has permanent four-wheel drive, which ensures power is sent to all four wheels continuously, on or off road. This also eliminates having to switch between two-wheel and four-wheel drive when conditions change, the car remains confident and secure in all types of terrain

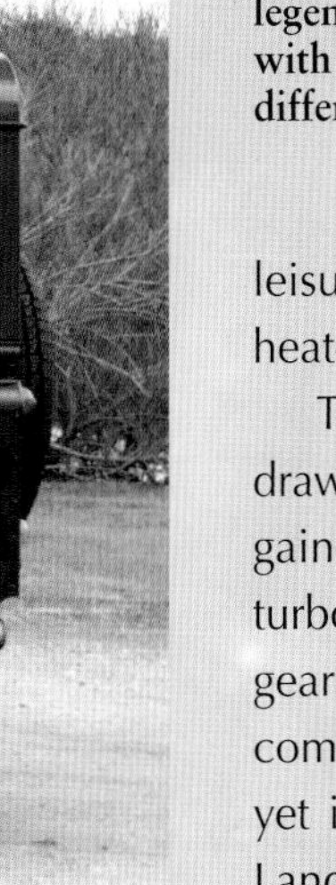

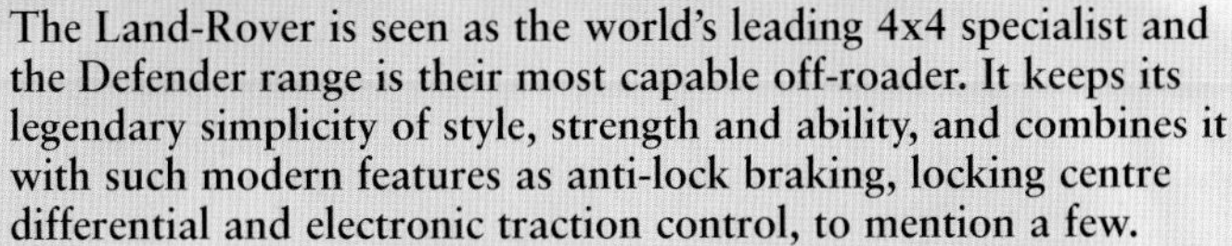

The Land-Rover is seen as the world's leading 4x4 specialist and the Defender range is their most capable off-roader. It keeps its legendary simplicity of style, strength and ability, and combines it with such modern features as anti-lock braking, locking centre differential and electronic traction control, to mention a few.

This vehicle's remarkably long life looked as though it was drawing to a close as the 2000s wore on, but new impetus was gained in 2007 when the Ford Transit's 2.4-litre four-cylinder turbo-diesel was fitted, together with such things as a six-speed gearbox and standard air conditioning. The Land-Rover had come a long way in 50 years. It was still clearly recognisable and yet it had an altogether more modern look. The four millionth Land-Rover was built in 2007 and a special SVX edition marked the model's 60th birthday in 2008, now as part of the Indian Tata group.

Lotus Seven

Few cars have remained in production for 50 years, but the Lotus Seven is one of them. Introduced in 1957 as only the second road car from Colin Chapman's still young company, it was still available, as a Caterham Seven, half a century later.

The first few Lotus models, from 1948 onwards, were Austin Seven-based trials specials. Their success prompted the development of the Mark 6, which although it still used proprietary running gear had its own unique chassis. Again this was very successful on the track and now also on the road, but it had been out of "production" for a while when economic reality convinced Chapman that he should build a successor.

The Mark Seven, always known in its spelt-out form, was conceived to keep the small factory team busy when they were not building the racing cars for which Lotus was gaining a reputation. In fact it was one of those racers, the Eleven, which provided the foundations for the Seven, although it bore a strong resemblance to the Mark Six.

Announced at the 1957 Earls Court Motor Show, the Seven was not actually in evidence, Chapman being much more interested in his new Elite coupé. With a tubular-steel spaceframe chassis carrying aluminium panels in a body that was every bit a

Featured here is a beautifully restored, Cheshunt-built Lotus Seven A. The series 1 Seven was built between September 1957 and June 1960. Approximately 243 in total, of which the first 100 (approximately) were built at 7, Tottenham Lane, Hornsey, London, whilst the remainder came from Delamare Road, Cheshunt, Hertfordshire, England.

The Series 1 had independent front suspension via transverse wishbones, incorporating anti-rollbar and utilising Standard 10 vertical links, Lotus design top arms by Quinton Hazell and Triumph TR3 steering arms. Springing was by combined coilspring damper units reacting through a single attachment point at each end.

two-seat racing car with lights and mudguards, the Seven could hardly have been simpler. Protection from the elements was little more than a gesture and bare polished aluminium was in abundance in the cockpit.

Under the skin, though, this car was born to perform. Power initially came from a 1172cc Ford side-valve engine with a three-speed gearbox. A BMC A-series option was mainly aimed at the USA. Racing double-wishbone suspension featured at the front, while the BMC rear axle was located by trailing arms and a Panhard rod. There were coil springs, telescopic dampers and disc brakes all round, while an old-style steering box was soon replaced by a rack-and-pinion system.

Most cars were sold in kit form. This roughly halved the price, mostly thanks to avoidance of the punitive purchase tax of the day. Any supplied instructions were deemed to negate this tax concession, so "repair" directions were included in the manual!

Road car this may have been, but it was soon sweeping the board on race tracks, to the point where rules were changed to hamper them and at one point in the 1970s Sevens were actually excluded – the resultant publicity slogan "Too fast to race" saying it all. For faster road use, the Super Seven of 1958 had a 1098cc light-alloy Coventry Climax engine, plus four gears and wire wheels. With an extra 37 bhp, this could manage over 160 kph (100 mph) and could reach 100 kph (60 mph) in 9 seconds.

A Series 2 mode was introduced in 1960. Costs (and weight) were reduced by removing some chassis tubes and the nosecone and wings (now integrated and flared at the front) were in glassfibre rather than aluminium. The Panhard rod was replaced by an A-bracket and Triumph front suspension components and steering gear were adopted.

The basic engine options were the same, but more, including the five-bearing Ford engine, were added to the list as time went

The all-aluminium-clad body had cycle type wings fitted over the front wheels. These were generally 15 x 4 in in diameter, lightweight, bolt-on steel rims with 520 x 15 in (crossply) tyres. This car has had alternative Dunlop wire wheels fitted (left and bottom).

Lotus Seven
1959

Engine:	In-line, four-cylinder, ohv
Power:	45 bhp @ 4500 rpm
Bore/stroke:	62.9 x 76.2 mm (2.48 x 3.0 in)
Capacity:	948 cc (57.9 cu in)
Transmission:	Rear drive, four gears
Wheelbase:	2235 mm (88 in)
Top speed:	128 kph (80 mph)

Period Les Leston steering wheel, new interior trim and correct instrumentation and switching is included on this car.

Shown here is the 948cc, BMC Mk I, AH Sprite A series engine, with twin H2 SU carburettors and Cooper air filters.

on. Front disc brakes also appeared for the first time in the Super Seven of 1962. It was during the 1960s that the Seven gained a considerable publicity boost, being chosen by Patrick McGoohan to feature in his TV series The Prisoner, which now enjoys cult status.

Lotus had lost interest in the Seven by this time, but Graham Nearn of sole distributor Caterham Car Sales kept the orders coming and the pressure on to develop the Seven further. The Series 3 appeared in 1968, with a wide range of minor improvements and – for the first time – the option of Lotus-Ford Twin Cam power, albeit with a strengthened chassis.

Lotus attempted to move the Seven into the lifestyle market – as well as to cut costs – with the glassfibre Series 4 of 1970. Altogether more civilised, the new car performed very well, but it lost its appeal to real enthusiasts and, although 1000 or more were made, did not gain enough new followers to move it into a new league. The last Lotus Seven was made in 1972, but Graham Nearn had done a deal with Lotus to take over production.

A few Caterham S4s were made, but in 1974 the Series 3 re-appeared, stiffened and fettled, but otherwise much as before and it has remained in production ever since – spawning quite a few clones. Engines and running gear, as always, have come from a variety of sources, often because the Seven has outlasted the "donor". Some cars have been extraordinarily fast. Top speed has

The basic shape of the Caterham Seven has changed little over the years but the engines it has used have. This is the 2008 Roadsport model and is seen as an all-rounder. Good on the track and also suitable for the road with plenty of protection from the elements for everyday driving.

The standard line-up of dials and instruments for the Caterham Seven is sufficient and essential. The dash can be upgraded to carbon and the front seats can be upgraded from cloth to leather also.

never been outstanding, through aerodynamic considerations, but some Caterham cars have broken records for acceleration to 100 and 160 kph.

Those taller than Colin Chapman's 1.7 m (5 ft 6 in) were pleased when a long-cockpit version was introduced in 1982 and de Dion rear suspension made a comeback, having featured on development cars.

The nearest thing to having a racing car for the road, the Seven remains true to its origins. Graham Nearn sold his company in 2005, but production continues unabated.

The front suspension comprises adjustable double wishbone with anti roll bar. The steering is managed via rack and pinion and the brakes are twin circuit split front/rear with low level warning system. Discs brakes are used front and rear.

The Roadsport 150 uses the latest Ford Sigma engine, which can accelerate the car from 0 to 96 kph (60 mph) in 5.0 seconds and gives it a top speed of 195 kph (122 mph).

The Roadsport is available with both the standard chassis, as seen here, and the wide-bodied "SV" chassis. The standard chassis has the familiar compact lightweight dimensions that have made the Seven a legend in its 50-year history.

Lotus Elan

The original Lotus Elan was launched at the end of 1962 to a rapturous reception from the Press. An inspired combination of timeless good looks, light weight, a healthy power output and nimble sure-footedness meant that it continued to inspire eulogy throughout its life. Yet had development continued along the planned lines, the Elan might have been a very different car.

Its elegant predecessor, the Elite, had itself created a storm, with its glassfibre monocoque under flowing lines and its ability to make the very most of the small engine's modest output. That

The car that became a legend, this is the Lotus Elan. This one in particular is special as it was the one that was given to one of the greatest racing drivers ever, Jim Clark, after he had won the world championship. Like many early Elans it did have its problems and it is understood that Clark was never very fond of it.

advanced construction brought its share of problems, not least stress cracks and excessive mechanical noise transmission. It was also very expensive to manufacture.

Lotus founder Colin Chapman was undeterred and worked towards designing a simpler monocoque for the Elite's successor, one that could be made in a single mould. This car was to be a two-plus-two and to make things really difficult it was to be a convertible, thus losing a substantial part of a closed car's innate rigidity. While a team lead by Ron Hickman (who later designed the Black & Decker Workmate) tackled this problem, Chapman

Lotus Elan 1962

Engine type	In-line four-cylinder, ohc
Power	105 bhp @ 5500 rpm
Bore/stroke	82.55 x 72.75 mm (3.25 x 2.86 in)
Capacity	1558cc (95.1cu in)
Transmission	Rear drive, four gears
Wheelbase	2134 mm (84.0 in)
Top speed	180 kph (112 mph)

To the left of the driver was the instrument panel, which accommodated the instrumentation and switches. The two handles at the top are pulled to open the bonnet.

Initially the Elan came as an open-top, two seater but from 1964 a fixed head coupé was also available. Both bodies were constructed from GRP and mounted on a separate chassis. The roof of the car featured is removable.

drew up a backbone chassis that could be used to try out his ideas for suspension.

As it turned out, that chassis, fabricated in sheet steel with a deep central backbone that divided into Y-sections at each end, had much more torsional rigidity than the Elite and the Formula One cars of the day. By happy accident, the problem was solved at a stroke. The prospect of low-cost construction meant that the Elite would be dropped and the new car would be another two-seater – for the moment at least.

Cost had also led Chapman to cast around for a cheaper engine than the Elite's race-derived Coventry Climax FWE. He knew that a five-bearing version of Ford's short-stroke four was on its way and he settled on this, but he wanted more sophistication than a pushrod engine could offer. His solution was to commission Harry Mundy, a highly respected engineer

Speedometer and tachometer are positioned in front of the driver and the wooden sports steering wheel.

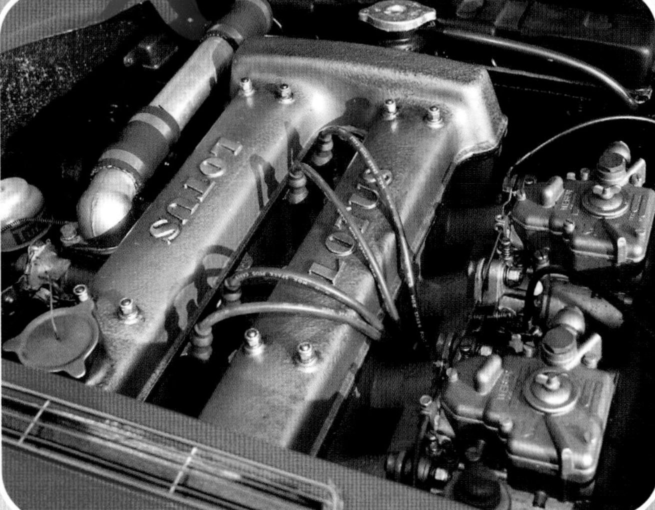

The initial 1500cc (91.53 cu in) engine was soon upgraded to 1558cc (95.1cu in). Note the twin-choke Weber carburettors on the right.

Headlights were housed in fibreglass pods and would be raised with the help of engine vacuum.

The twin-cam engine fitted to the Lotus Elan S3.

who was then working as *Autocar* magazine's Technical Editor, to design a new overhead-cam cylinder head. This he did to remarkable effect, and the famous Twin Cam was born.

Equipped with two twin-choke Weber carburettors, the aluminium head was tried on various-capacity versions of the Ford bottom end, but 1.5 litres was settled on for the launch, with a quoted power output of 100 bhp. In fact only 22 Elans were built with this before it was enlarged to 1558cc with a view to using it in 1.6-litre racing classes. Power output was now officially 105 bhp at 5500 rpm, although later Lotus workshop manuals had it as just 90 bhp.

A Ford four-speed gearbox was used, with semi-close ratios, and delightfully direct gear-change with the short lever mounted on top of a high transmission tunnel. A short propeller shaft drove

The Elan was the first Lotus road car to use the now famous steel backbone chassis with a fibreglass body. At 1500 lb (680 kg), the Elan embodied the Colin Chapman minimum weight design philosophy.

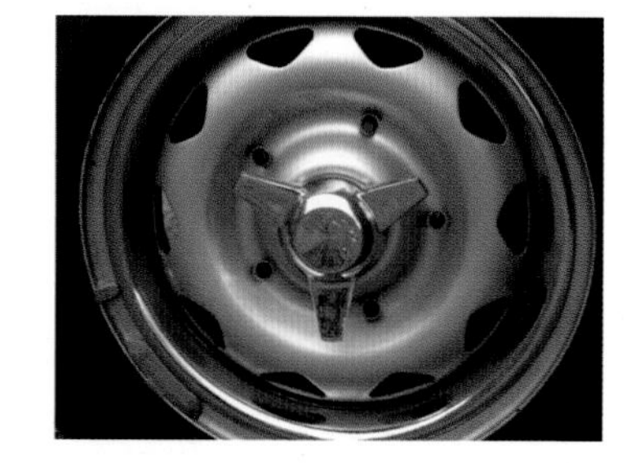

Seen from above the little Elan S3 is elegant and pretty. Get behind the wheel and it really does take your breath away. Steel wheels were standard – shown here are the centre-lock type.

A view inside the cab of a 1969 S4 hardtop Elan, showing the wooden dashboard and comfortable sports seats.

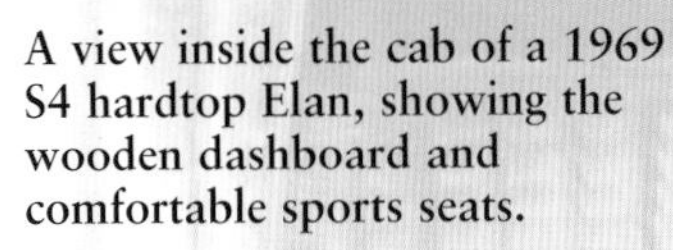

The bulge in the bonnet of the S4 was added so as to be able to fit the Stromberg carburettors.

Stromberg CD carburettors were originally installed in order to meet US emission requirements but were adopted for some British S4s for a short period.

The fourth series of the Elan bought some refinements – the most obvious here is the flaring of the wheel arches and the new larger rear lights.

the rear wheels via a chassis-mounted final drive and open drive shafts fitted with Rotoflex rubber universal couplings.

The suspension was independent all round, with double wishbones and coil spring/damper units. There was an anti-roll bar at the front and a modified Chapman strut layout at the rear, with a rigid spring/damper and a wide-based lower wishbone on each side. It was the relatively soft settings coupled with long travel that gave the Elan its remarkable combination of road-holding, handling and ride comfort. Brakes were discs all round and after a short while centre-lock steel wheels were standard.

The pretty body had plenty of room for two, plus a little stowage space behind the seats, as well as a useful boot. Its shape was made even more attractive by the use of pop-up headlamps and, in typical style, Chapman made use of the front chassis cross-member as a reservoir for the engine-created vacuum that was used to operate these.

By the standards of the day, the Elan, or Lotus 26, was very advanced. The admittedly cheaper MGB was also introduced in 1962, for instance, and it had a pushrod engine, a live rear axle, rear drum brakes and antiquated lever arm dampers. In a straight

The Elan Plus 2 also had the vacuum-operated headlights but these were fitted into the bonnet rather than in the wings.

The Elan Plus 2S 130, was presented in 1971 and could easily be distinguished from its basic brother by the silver roof. Under the bonnet was the 126 bhp "Big-Valve" engine, which could rush the car to 60 mph (96 kph) in a little over 7 seconds.

line, the Lotus could reach 100 kph (60 mph) in under 9 seconds and go on to a top speed of 180 kph (112 mph). And it could corner and stop to match.

To keep the price down, Lotus offered the Elan as a kit, which in practice meant fitting parts such as suspension and engine in order to avoid a crippling purchase tax. The factory provided a free checking service for those who undertook their own finishing.

A Series 2 version appeared in 1964, with minor modifications, such as new rear lamp clusters. Shortly afterwards, the powerful Special Equipment edition was introduced. With new camshafts, this had a quoted 115 bhp. More major changes came with the S3 of 1966. This had electric windows and a new wrap-around boot lid and a folding rather than lift-off hood. The fixed-head coupé that was by now available already had these improvements, while a more refined Ford gearbox, from the Corsair 200E, was not standard.

The rear lights were changed again for the S4 of 1968, which also had modified wheel arches and, for a short while, Stromberg carburettors, but the final two-seat Elan was probably the best. Introduced in 1971, the S4 Sprint had a re-worked big-valve version of the Twin Cam, with Dell'Orto carburettors, which produced a genuine 126 bhp and took the car to 100 kph (60 mph) in under 7 seconds and then on to 193 kph (120 mph).

The interior of the Plus 2 was certainly more comfortable than its two-seater stablemate. All the same, getting anybody into the rear seats proved a problem, even young children. Small touches had made the interior friendlier and a little bit more sophisticated.

A 1972 Elan Sprint – two tone paintwork and the stripe that tells the story. This car never lacked speed or excitement.

The powerplant of one of the last Elan Sprints to come out of the factory. This is a stage III, 150 bhp QED-built motor and the carburettors are Dell'Orto, as fitted to late Elans from new.

The introduction of VAT in 1973 put paid to the fiscal benefits of kit cars and Lotus saw its future as being further up market. The last of 12,200 two-seat Elans left the factory in August that year, but the Elan Plus 2, which had been introduced in 1967, continued into 1974.

Unmistakably the Elan's big brother, the Plus 2 was 584 mm (23 in) longer and 254 mm (10 in) wider, but only 25 mm (1 in) higher, so that if anything it appeared to be even sleeker. It was mechanically identical to the two-seater, but the chassis was extended to accommodate two child-sized rear seats. There was never an official drop-head version of the stretched car, which came with the SE engine and wider wheels and tyres.

The Plus 2S of late 1968 had cosmetic refinements, but it was in 1971 that the car really gained its wings. The Plus 2S 130 had the big-valve engine and was about as fast as the Sprint, although the 130 of the name was optimistic. The final version, known as the 130/5 at last had a five-speed gearbox (which was also fitted to one or two two-seaters right at the end). This brought great touring refinement, which kept the Plus 2 in production until the end of 1974, by which time 5200 of these Elans had been built.

In its final form, the Elan Sprint is a desirable car and can fetch a good price if in good condition.

MG T series

When the first of the MG T-series models, the TA Midget, was unveiled in 1936, it was seen by many as a step backwards from the competition-developed overhead-cam PB. And yet it and its successors lasted for nearly 20 years and came to typify the traditional British sports car.

Lord Nuffield had sold his privately owned MG Car Company to the publicly quoted Morris Motors of which he was also head. He pronounced that the design department at MG's Abingdon factory would close and that all future MGs should make full use of the parts bins at the main Cowley factory and should be suitable for low-cost production. Founder and driving force Cecil Kimber was effectively demoted and, as commanded, the TA

The MG TA replaced the older PB model in 1936 and like it, most were two seat open cars with a steel body on an ash frame (below). Throughout the T series, the cars were equipped with a spare wheel that was fixed to the rear of the car (right).

The TA was an evolution of the previous car and was 3 inches (76 mm) wider in its track and 7 inches (180 mm) longer in its wheelbase. The previous advanced overhead cam engine was replaced by a more typical MPJG, overhead valve unit from the Wolseley 10 but with twin SU carburettors, modified camshaft and manifold.

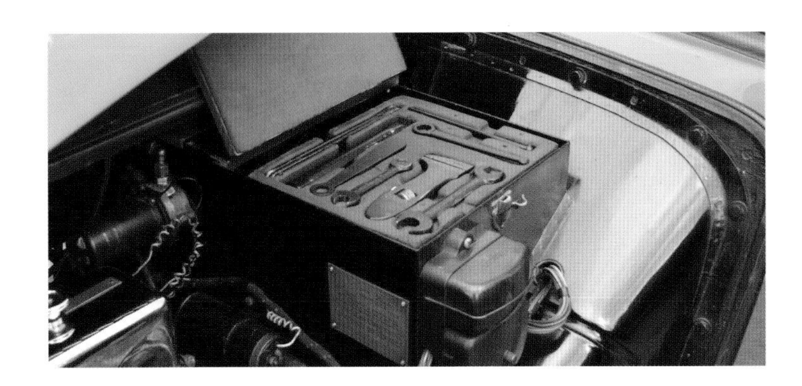

borrowed its pushrod engine from the Wolseley Ten and shared many other parts with models from the Nuffield Organisation.

The new car was bigger than its predecessors, although its construction was similar. The channel-section chassis, which was completely boxed around the engine bay, carried beam axles at front and rear, hung on leaf springs. The engine itself had a capacity of 1292cc, considerably larger than the PB's 939cc unit, and produced over 50 bhp, which was sufficient to give the heavier TA comparable performance. Hydraulically operated drum brakes were fitted all round.

Open two-seater bodywork with steel panels on ash framing was standard, the flowing front wings giving this Midget a definite sporting style. There were also two, more expensive

Although the instrumentation was comprehensive, it was laid out so that the driver had the tachometer in front of him rather than the speedometer (above). Much more importance was put on the rev limits in those days, unlike today when speed limits are so much more governed. A tool kit was provided, not just on one side of the engine compartment but both (above left). Another similar selection to this is under the other side.

The TC was the first post-war MG and was launched in 1945.

options: the Airline Coupé, built by Carbodies of Coventry, and carried over from the PB, and a Tickford drophead coupé, which with a smaller price premium was the more popular.

Viewed with suspicion by MG connoisseurs, the TA actually proved in magazine tests to be quite competent, with a top speed of around 129 kph (80 mph). Sales soon began to pick up, even without the benefit of works competition efforts, which had also been banned in the shake-up. The ban did not prevent the Abingdon team from preparing special lightweight tuned TAs for customers, and several of these were very successful in trials and track events.

Just before war broke out a new T-type arrived, even though it was hardly publicised. The TB looked the same as the TA, but it had a new engine and gearbox. At 1250cc, the XPAG overhead-valve four had roughly the same capacity as the earlier unit, but its bores were bigger and its stroke shorter, which made it more responsive and slightly more powerful. It also had a much better – dry-plate – clutch and a new gearbox with synchromesh on the upper three of the four ratios. Synchronisation had appeared on later TAs but only on third and top.

The TB was short-lived. When war came, all car production ceased, with only 379 TBs built, compared with 3,003 TAs.

With post-war shortages, MG concentrated on a one-model policy in 1945 and it was a new Midget that took this honour, appearing just five weeks after the official end of hostilities. For

The TC was quite similar to the pre-war TB, sharing the same engine (right) but with a slightly higher compression ratio of 7.4:1 giving 54.5 bhp at 5200 rpm. No doubting where this car was made – a metal strip is often placed at the bottom of the door enclosure to denote the company (above).

By using more modern elements for the interior of the car, quite a lot of space was gained, giving the driver and passenger more room.

A beautifully restored and kept TC. Although some were exported to the United States, they were only built as a right-hand drive.

Smaller 15-inch (380-mm) disc type road wheels were now added, whilst bumpers and over-riders became standard for the first time. The car was also 5 inches (130 mm) wider with a track of 50 inches (1300 mm).

The 1950 TD combined the TCs drivetrain, but with modified rear axle, with the MG Y-type chassis and familiar T-type style body. An independent suspension using coil springs in front was new as were rack and pinion steering.

Nearly 30,000 TDs had been produced, including about 1700 Mk II models, when the series ended in 1953 with all but 1656 exported.

what was known as the TC, modifications to the rear spring mountings, which now had rubber bushes for a smoother ride, allowed greater body width across the cockpit, which also had a new instrument display. There were one or two other very minor changes, but in other ways the TC was identical to the TB, albeit now with no optional body styles.

Although it was anything but new, the TC was a winner, sales quickly picking up. This was the T-type that really attracted interest in the United States for the first time, even though the special American edition retained right-hand drive. More than any other, the TC was the model that established a craze in the USA for British sports cars. Of 10,000 TCs built, around two-thirds went abroad, although only 2001 of them found their way to America.

The 1250cc engine was very responsive to tuning and many TCs were to be seen on the race tracks of the world. A special-bodied version ran twice in the Le Mans 24-hour race and one was even entered for the 1949 French Grand Prix, which was a sports car event that year.

The company did not rest on its laurels. Despite its popularity, the TC was now a very old-fashioned car. Separate chassis were still common enough in open cars, but ash framing for the

This is a 1953 convertible. The hood sits quite high and gives the occupants plenty of headroom, although the car looks a lot better with the hood down.

By now the tachometer had joined the speedometer and both were positioned in front of the driver. Other knobs and dials are also nearby.

MG Midget TD 1953

Engine type	In-line, four-cylinder, overhead valve
Power	54 bhp @ 5200 rpm
Bore/stroke	66.5 x 90mm (2.62 x 3.54 in)
Capacity	1250cc (76.3 cu in)
Transmission	Rear drive, four gears
Wheelbase	2388 mm (94.0 in)
Top speed	133 kph (83 mph)

The engine and transmission of the TD were again the same as the TC – the now familiar twin-carburettor, 1250cc (76.28 cu in), pushrod, XPAG unit.

panelling was largely outmoded and a leaf-sprung solid front axle was decidedly vintage. A heater was not even an optional extra.

The TD, which came in 1949, looked very similar – indeed the prototype used a TC body – but it made a few concessions to modern expectations. The chassis was now a shortened version of that from the Y-type saloon, with box-section members and, for the first time, independent front suspension. This had wishbones and coil springs and was combined with advanced rack-and-pinion steering, which meant that the TD could easily be made in left-hand drive form. The gearbox, too, came from the Y-type, as did the steel wheels that replaced the earlier spoked items. More powerful brakes gave greater stopping power.

The wheelbase was unaltered, but the track was wider and the bodywork was extended to suit, with chrome-plated front bumpers added front and rear. This made the TD look more different than it actually was. Despite greater weight, lower gearing kept performance close to the TCs and the TD was soon outselling its predecessor. In its four-year life it was the best-selling T-type of all, with more than 29,600 cars sold, 32 of them abroad for every one in the UK.

A Mark II TD was built with competition in mind. A special cylinder head and increased compression ratio boosted the power output, and some success was achieved, but sales started to decline as the MG's age began to show itself against a new breed of sports cars.

A new two-seater was on the drawing board in 1952, but it did not get beyond the prototype stage before the formation of BMC brought Austin and its new Austin Healey into the corporation and put the project on hold. In an effort to keep the

T series alive, the TD was hurriedly face-lifted for the 1953 London Motor Show. The scuttle height was reduced, a new sloping grille introduced, the wings made more integrated and the headlamps built in, but underneath it was very much as before, with a slightly detuned version of the Mark II TD engine. Wire wheels returned as an option and there were improved seats, as part of a major interior redesign, which included a heater for the first time.

A 1466cc engine was introduced in 1954, with enlarged bores and 63 bhp. This gave the TF a top speed of 142 kph (88 mph). Unpopular with purists, it was undoubtedly the best of the Ts and is now highly sought after. Sales at 9600 were better than might have been expected, but the arrival of the MGA in 1955 finally brought the run to an end.

By the early 1950s, sales of the TD were starting to fall back and it needed an injection of some sort to revive interest. Sadly, all that came out was cosmetic and so it was that the TF appeared in 1953 (above). Basically the new car had the same form of chassis, suspension, brakes, steering, engine, and transmission, although some change had taken place with the instrumentation (right).

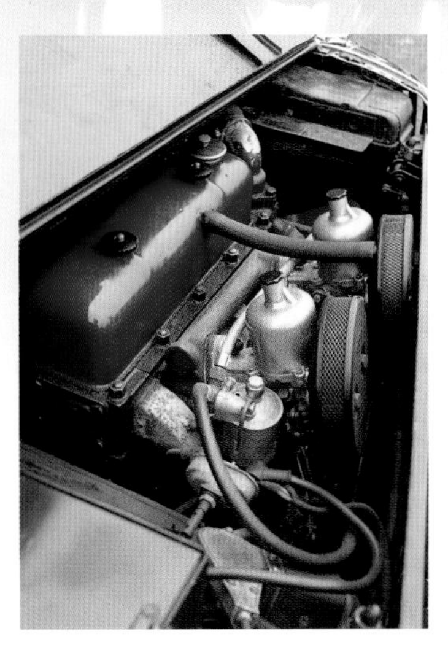

Even with all this cosmetic upgrade, in terms of performance there was no change in comparison with the TD and sales figures still looked unfavourable. The tired old 1250 cc (76.28 cu in) engine (left) was eventually increased in size but even that didn't help the cause.

It was in the bodywork that most changes had taken place. The radiator grille had been lowered and raked to give a lower hood line and the front wings were shaped so that the headlights could be faired into them rather than being separately mounted.

MGA

Although the steering wheel, which is made of aluminium and wood, is not original, it is a welcome addition. The remainder of the instruments though, are original.

The MGA should have appeared several years earlier than it did, but its launch was delayed by the Austin Healey 100 being introduced by the newly constituted BMC, of which MG was a part, in 1952. When it did finally make the showrooms in 1955, it moved the company firmly into the modern era.

The outgoing TF Midget, introduced as a stop-gap when the MGA was put on hold, was very old fashioned, both in looks and in construction. The new car was equipped to take on the popular rivals of the day, such as the Triumph TR2 and even the more powerful Jaguar XK120. Based on some of MG's recent racers, the A was built to blend performance with practicality.

A box-section steel perimeter chassis carried the pressed-steel bodywork and allowed the seats to be mounted low between its

When the MGA arrived in 1955, its modern and curvaceous new bodywork must have taken the MG aficionados a little by surprise. Featured here is a beautiful 1960 MGA Mk I. This particular car went though a 6-year rebuild to bring it back to this close-to-original condition.

Shortly after the introduction of the MGA Twin Cam, the standard cars were also given a 1588cc (96.9 cu in) version of the standard pushrod B-series engine (above) and became known as the MGA 1600. The 1600 continued to be offered in both open (right) and coupé versions. They were also equipped with disc brakes on the front wheels, but continued with drums at the rear.

The rear light clusters on the MGA also tell a tale. The 1500 models have a smaller plinth than the one shown, the 1600 models are as the one in the picture and 1622 models have them positioned horizontally.

The new MGA also saw a shortened, stylised and widened variation of the now familiar MG grille.

main members. A world away from the TF's vintage style, this open two-seater was smooth and sleek, with an aerodynamic efficiency that made it considerably faster than the TF with an engine of the same size. It also offered reasonable luggage space for a car of this type, although the majority of the boot space was taken up by the spare wheel and a boot lid rack was a popular option.

The engine was a 1498cc B-series unit, with four cylinders, pushrod-operated overhead valves and twin SU carburettors. It developed 68 bhp at first (soon to go up to 72 bhp) and with a four-speed gearbox it gave the A a top speed of almost 160 kph (100 mph) and acceleration to 100 kph (60 mph) in around 15 seconds.

The front suspension had wishbones and coil springs and the rear semi-elliptic leaf springs, with lever-arm dampers, in a similar layout to the TF. Rack-and-pinion steering gave good response, while the brakes were drums, also taken from the TF.

The MGA was an immediate hit. More of these were built in the model's best year, 1959, than of all MGs up to the war. It was fast and it handled and stopped well. It was also reasonably comfortable, although inevitably bumpy, and much more roomy than the narrow-bodied T-types. For those wanting more comfort,

The MGA Twin Cam, introduced in 1958, was aimed particularly at those who wanted to compete in racing events, rather than for everyday use. Outwardly, there was little to distinguish it from the standard models, except perhaps the centre-locking wheels. Inwardly, this was a different animal.

a fixed-head coupé was added in 1956, with wind-up windows and a large, curved windscreen.

If the 1500cc engine was not enough, after July 1958 speed seekers could opt for the MGA Twin Cam. A special cylinder head had been developed for an overbored 1588cc version of the B-series engine. To cope with the 108 bhp that this produced, the Twin Cam had disc brakes all round. It also sported centre-lock steel wheels. With 50 per cent more power than the 1500 A, the Twin Cam could reach 185 kph (115 mph), although the

Little had also changed to the instruments and their positioning on the MGA Twin Cam.

unusually high compression ratio of 9.9:1 meant that the engine had to be treated carefully and fed only with five-star fuel. Failures, especially in the American market, led to this model's sudden cancellation in 1960, although by then the compression ratio had been reduced and the problem solved. It was a sad end for a promising engine that in its undeveloped form was not suited to use by the mechanically unaware or unsympathetic.

By this time, the standard cars shared the 1588cc capacity, which made them a little faster, with power up to 80 bhp. They also had front disc brakes and featured improvements to the hood and sidescreens.

The cylinder bore size and thus engine capacity went up again in 1961, when the MGA acquired Mark II status. The new size was 1622cc, which was only a little larger, but the block and head were very much changed, with bigger inlet valves and a new crankshaft, pistons, con-rods and flywheel. Power was now 86 bhp but higher gearing kept performance much the same, if more relaxed. A new radiator grille and horizontal rear light clusters distinguished the MkII from the outside.

Left-over Twin Cam bodies were converted into what were known as De Luxe models. These had Twin Cam equipment, but were powered first by the 1588cc pushrod engine and then, in MkII form, by the 1622cc unit. Only 395 of these were made. Total production of the MGA was over 101,000, of which a staggering 95,000 or so went abroad. When production finished in 1962, it was to make way for the MGB, an altogether more modern car.

A nice touch – there is nothing quite like polished aluminium – this is one of the two cam covers which had the MG logo embossed on them.

Although there were a lot of cosmetic changes little happened in the driver's compartment.

MGA Twin Cam
1959

Engine type	In-line, four-cylinder, dohc
Power	108 bhp @ 6700 rpm
Bore/stroke	75.4 x 88.9 mm (3.0 x 3.5 in)
Capacity	1588cc (96.9cu in)
Transmission	Rear drive, four gears
Wheelbase	2380 mm (94 in)
Top speed	185 kph (115 mph)

The MGA Twin Cam could speed to a maximum approaching 185 kph (115 mph) and acceleration times were cut by a considerable amount too, compared to the standard car. With the speeds being attained and acceleration being used, it seemed only sensible that the car should have four-wheel disc brakes.

This is the heart of where all the significant changes were made – the engine was basically a development of the B-series unit which was being used in the standard car. Essentially, the cylinder block and bottom end were strengthened B-series components, but the cylinder head was a new aluminium unit incorporating twin overhead camshafts and twin SU carburettors were fitted as standard.

MGB

Work on what was to be the last new MG sports car until the mid-engined F-type was introduced in 1995 began before the last version of the MGA had been announced, back in the late 1950s. The first effort had an Italian Frua body mounted on an MGA chassis, but this did not win favour and it was one of Abingdon's own draughtsmen, with some assistance from Pininfarina, who designed the gentle yet elegant curves of the MGB.

Slightly shorter and wider than the A, the B was much roomier. This was largely thanks to the fact that it had dispensed

The boot area housed the spare wheel in a well and the tool kit in its bag along with the jack. Seen here also are some essentials that were handy to have in the car – a new fan belt, a first aid kit, a spare oil filter and of course a workshop manual.

Reputed to be the oldest surviving MGB in the UK, this is a concours winner. It has been lovingly restored to its original spec and regularly attends shows, where it walks off with the top trophies.

The interior of the car had leather seats, black-crackle dash with cable-drive tachometer and a large 16 inch (406.4 mm) steering wheel with three spokes and a central horn-push.

with a separate chassis, having instead a unitary steel body/chassis construction with an aluminium bonnet panel. Launched in the autumn of 1962, the MGB was powered by the B-series engine that had been carried over from the A, but bored out to take it from 1622 to 1798cc in an effort to ensure that the B was faster despite being heavier than the car it was replacing. A pushrod four, the basics of this unit had been around since 1949, and with twin SU carburettors it now developed 95 bhp.

The four-speed gearbox had no synchromesh on first gear, but it did soon gain the option of overdrive, which helped to give relaxed cruising in the days when a fourth gear was a luxury, never mind the fifth that is the minimum now. The B was technically old-fashioned when it was announced, in that the rear wheels were driven through a live axle which sat on leaf springs. The front was independent, with wishbones, coil springs and a strangely optional anti-

MGB

1962

Engine type	In-line four cylinder, ohv
Power	95 bhp @ 5400 rpm
Bore/stroke	80.26 x 88.9 mm (3.16 x 3.5 in)
Capacity	1798cc (109.7 cu in)
Transmission	Rear drive, four gears
Wheelbase	2311 mm (91 in)
Top speed	173 kph (108 mph)

The original 1962 car was supplied with pressed-steel wheels, as shown here, or there was the option of centre-locking wire wheels.

The engine and transmission of the first production cars were that of the the MGA, although the B series engine was increased in capacity to 1798cc (109.7 cu in).

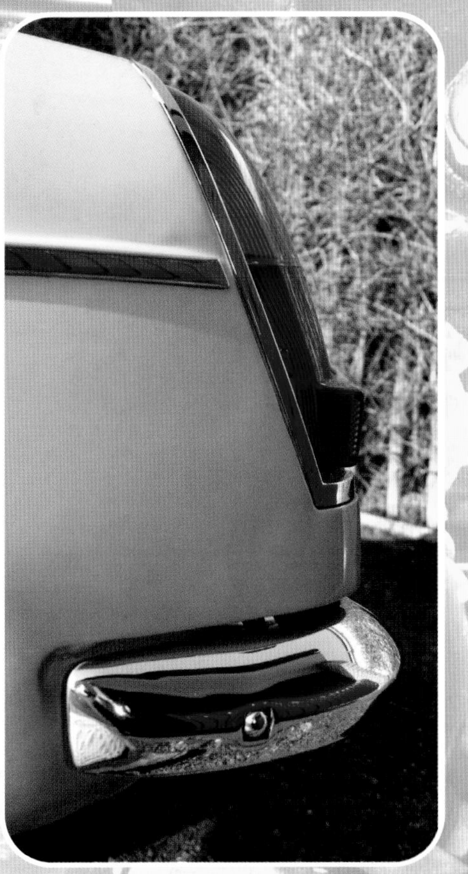

The rear lights were neatly sculpted into the rear wings.

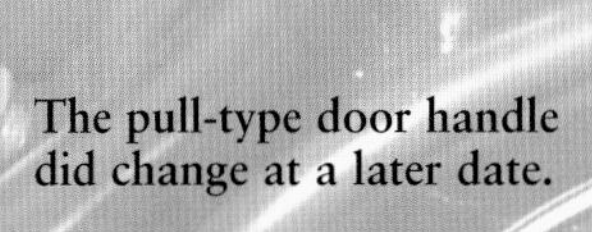

The pull-type door handle did change at a later date.

This is a 1967 vintage Mk I MGB that has recently been restored to its former glory.

From late 1964 the Mk I had received a new engine with five main bearings and an oil cooler was a standard fit for UK cars.

Although there had been minor trim changes, the interior of the 1967 car had not changed a great deal, but the tachometer was now electronic. The steering wheel shown is not standard.

Taking into account the period, the MGB was a handsome looking sports car and certainly ahead of its time. The top speed of 160 kph (100 mph) was quite something and hitting the magical "ton" was quite a thrill.

roll bar, but antiquated lever-arm dampers had to do duty at each corner. This was a layout that was largely responsible for the B being dubbed a Morris Oxford drop-head by the unconverted. Nonetheless, at least front disc brakes were standard and there was a choice of steel or wire wheels, while steering was by rack and pinion.

From the start the MGB was a big seller, attracting much more interest than any previous MG sports car had done. As usual, the bulk of production was destined for foreign shores, not least for America, whose demands were to influence the shape of Bs to come. Before that, though, the engine gained a stronger five-bearing crankshaft in 1964. The power output was unchanged, but the engine was considered by some to be less lively. Acceleration to 100 kph (60 mph) took around 12 seconds and the top speed was a little under 177 kph (110 mph).

The interior had changed little but now there was a collapsible steering column. The US version had a padded dashboard with no glove compartment.

A hard top was already available, but in 1965 a closed coupé version known as the GT was introduced. A taller windscreen accompanied a fixed roof that extended to a sloping and opening rear window. Heavier than the convertible, this was also more aerodynamic and thus slightly faster. It also had a small rear seat that could just about carry two children.

The Mark II MGB of 1967 brought some significant improvements. The standard gearbox now had synchromesh on first and there was an optional three-speed automatic for the first time, which was intended to appeal to GT customers. That year also saw the announcement of the MGC, which had the Austin Healey 3000's 3-litre six squeezed under its bulging bonnet. The

The MGB Mk II was introduced in late 1967. There was a new all-synchromesh gearbox with an automatic box as an optional extra. Wire wheels were optional too, the standard fit being four-stud, painted, steel Rostyle wheels from 1969.

By late 1970 the bumper over-riders had been fitted with black plastic facings. A roadster never looks quite right with the hood up, it doesn't seem natural.

extra weight demanded new torsion bar front suspension and uprated braking. The C was never popular and was dropped in 1969, with 9000 roadsters and GTs built.

Further changes were made in production as the years passed, with such things as Rostyle steel wheels, modified rear lights, a recessed black grille and interior revisions. The biggest update came with the introduction of the MGB GT V8 in 1973. Inspired by specialist converted cars, this used Rover's 3.5-litre V8 engine, whose 137 bhp gave this B a top speed of 201 kph (125 mph) and a 0–100 kph (0–60 mph) time of 7.7 seconds. Being all aluminium, the V8 was roughly the same weight as the B-series engine so handling was unaffected, but the car was surprisingly never a good seller, perhaps in part because no drop-head was

From this angle you could be forgiven for thinking this was just an MGB GT, there is little to tell you that this is the V8 version. On closer inspection you might notice the badge on the grille and you would certainly know if the engine was started. Many of the V8s had the US style rubber bumper – even though they were never officially sold there – but this one has kept the chrome type with rubber ends on the over-riders.

Under the bonnet, the V8 transforms the space into a mass of engine components. The Buick-designed Rover 3.5-litre takes over the compartment, yet because it is so flat, there is no need for bumps and bulges in the bonnet. This particular owner has swapped the original air filter system for a more sporty version.

The cabin of the V8 is luxurious, with plush carpets, leather seats and walnut dash. It can get quite hot in the cabin though, with the heat of the big engine wafting in from the engine compartment just ahead.

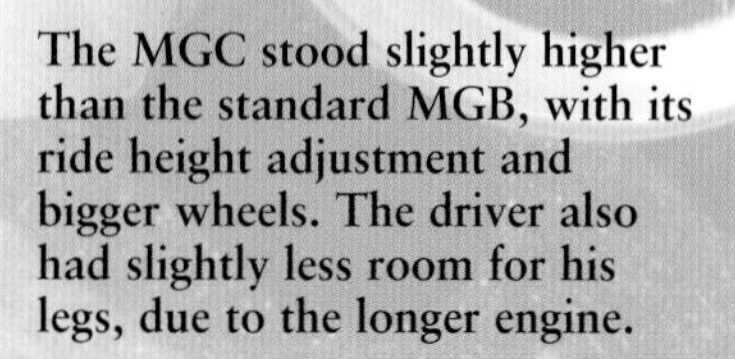

The MGC stood slightly higher than the standard MGB, with its ride height adjustment and bigger wheels. The driver also had slightly less room for his legs, due to the longer engine.

available, and only 2591 were sold before this type was dropped in 1976.

By this time, the American influence had taken over and the 1974 revision to the range had brought an increased ride height and ugly rubber impact-absorbing bumpers. A steel bonnet lid added to the already greater weight and the handling was compromised until a rear anti-roll bar was added and the front one stiffened in 1976.

The MGB soldiered on in this form until 1980, when the Abingdon factory closed and the last car was made. More than 520,000 Bs had left those historic works, nearly 400,000 of them roadsters.

The last two cars to drift off the production line at Abingdon were a roadster and a GT and both were Special Edition models. Seen here is that last GT, now housed at the Heritage Motor Museum in Gaydon, England.

Announced late in 1976, the MGC (above) could be recognised quite easily with its substantial bulge in the bonnet. This was needed to accommodate its 3-litre, six-cylinder engine (top).

Equipped with US style bumpers, polished ring-centre wheels and side flashes, this Special Edition MGB GT saw the end of the Abingdon factory and with it the end of the MGB.

Morgan three-wheelers

Harry Morgan, better known by his initials HFS, did not have commercial motor manufacture in mind when he built himself a cyclecar in 1909. A simple device, with a Peugeot engine, this was intended for his own use. Yet it attracted considerable interest, and a century later the company he founded as a result is still owned by his family and produces some of the world's most famous cars in the shadow of Worcestershire's Malvern Hills.

That little machine set the style for all the Morgan three-wheelers that followed. In the more stable of the two possible configurations, there were two wheels at the front and one at the back. The front suspension was independent and already used a sliding pillar system that was soon to be patented and to appear

The first Runabout was produced back in 1910, was a single seater and used a Peugeot engine. After much development and sporting acclaim, a Sporting Runabout was presented in 1914. This used a JAP, sidevalve, air-cooled, 964cc (58.82 cu in) engine, equipped with a two forward-speed gearbox with no reverse.

on Morgans right up to the present day. The rear wheel was suspended on the ends of two quarter-elliptic springs.

The first single-seaters were displayed at the Olympia Cycle & Motor Cycle Exhibition of 1910, with single- and twin-cylinder engines, but HFS soon realised that there was a bigger market for two-seaters. He had soon made the necessary changes and now seats were side by side. He also competed with great success in the Exeter Trial of 1910, which brought more enquiries.

A tubular chassis formed the foundation for the minimal bodywork. The engine was mounted at the front and drive to the two-speed gearbox at the back was by a shaft fitted into one of the chassis tubes. The two gear ratios were provided by two final drive chains with different-sized sprockets. The rear wheel also had the Morgan's only brake.

This was the basis for all Morgans for the next few years. The Morgan Motor Company was established in 1912 with HFS as Managing Director and his father, the Reverend Prebendary HG Morgan, as Chairman. The Malvern works was soon assembling several different variations on the theme. The De Luxe had better bodywork and equipment than the Standard and victory in the Amiens Cyclecar Grand Prix of 1913 gave rise to a replica that was capable of 97 kph (60 mph).

During the First World War, the factory concentrated on the munitions effort, but some three-wheelers were still made and HFS built his first four-seater, albeit for his own family's use at that stage. The layout of the little cars might have been constant, but the company used a variety of engines over the next decade or so, usually V-twins, mounted either ahead of the body or behind a rudimentary cowling in more car-like style.

Although the four-seater did go into production after the war, there was also a Family model, which was a two-seater with a luggage locker. In addition, there was also a Sports Family model, which had the frontal appearance of the Sports model but was like the Family at the rear.

The round-tailed Aero of the early 1920s took its name from the two small "aero" screens in place of the full-width type. With

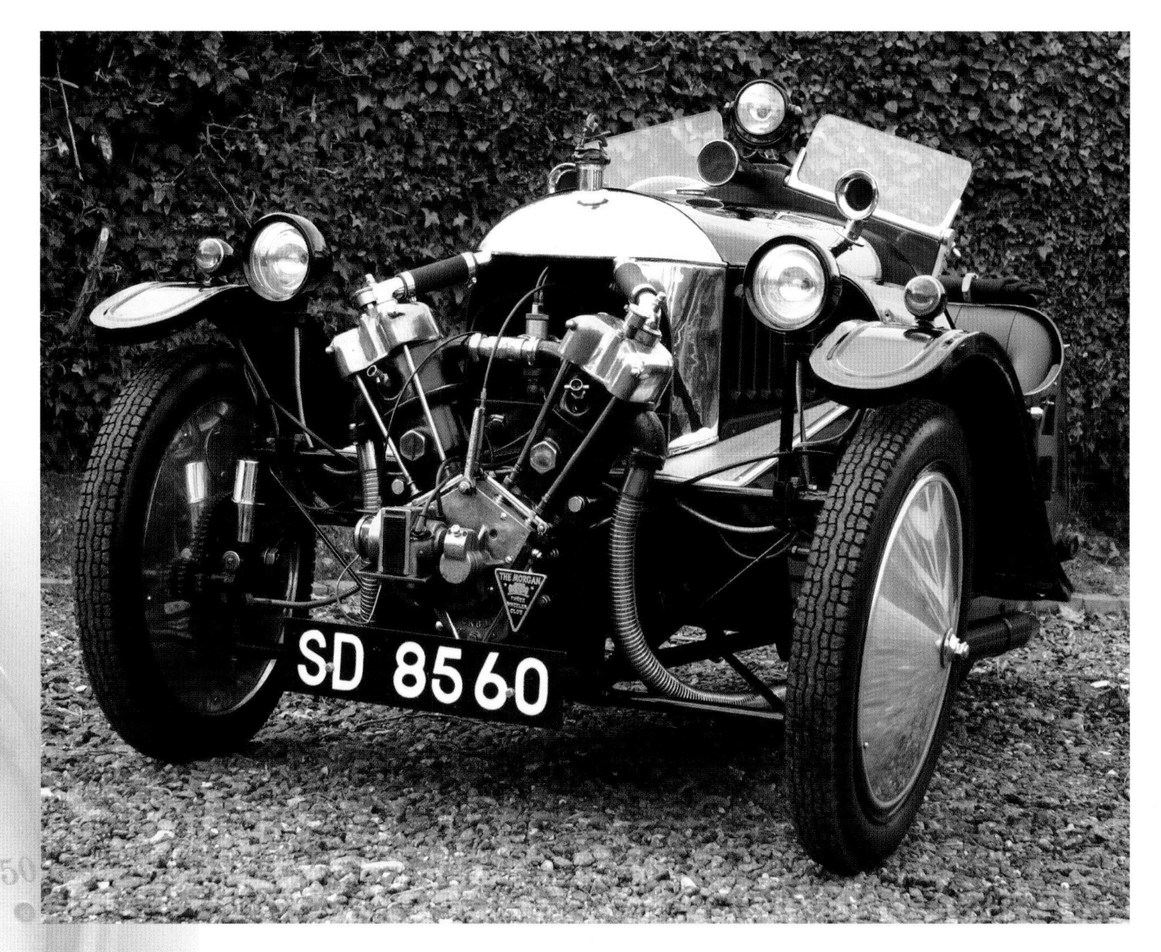

Although listed for the first time in the Morgan sales catalogue for 1920, it is understood that some Aeros had been built prior to that date. Featured here (above and right) is a 1924 example, which has a Blackburn engine of 1098cc (67 cu in). The engine is an overhead valve model, is water cooled and uses a 2-speed gearbox.

Controls and instruments – of what there was – for the Runabout, were neatly positioned on the firewall, away from the elements.

Looking a little like a nightmare today, this is the steering wheel and controls for the 1934 Supersport model. The small lever on the left controlled the advance and retard for the ignition. The larger lever on the right acted as a throttle and the smaller lever acted as a choke and controlled the air.

A close-up view between the two cylinders showing the Amal carburettor with its two float chambers.

Surprisingly the windscreen wiper was a standard fit at this stage. It worked from the vacuum of the inlet manifold.

Morgan Super Sports 1934

Engine type	V-twin, ohv
Power	39 bhp
Bore/stroke	85.5 x 85.5 mm (3.37 x 3.37 in)
Capacity	990cc (60.41cu in)
Transmission	Rear drive, three gears
Wheelbase	2209 mm (87 in)
Top speed	120 kph (75 mph)

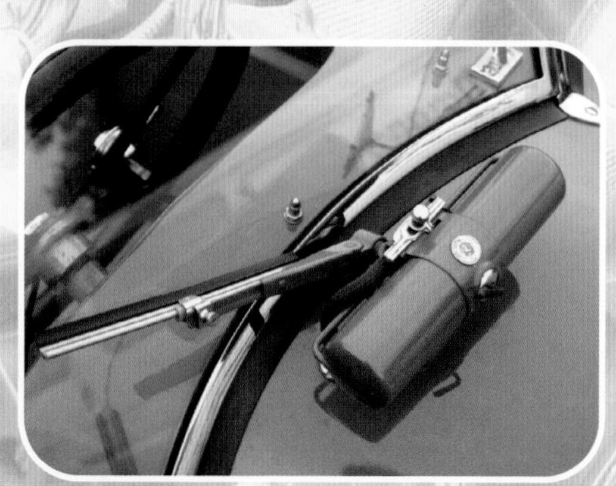

Front independent suspension consisted of Morgan sliding pillar with hydraulic dampers. The front brakes were hand operated whilst the rear were foot operated.

The spare wheel looked a little clumsy stuck on the rear of the F4, but possibly no less so than being put on the top of the rear of the bodywork.

In 1927 Morgan built an Aero with a tuned engine and modified bodywork – it was called a Super Sports Aero or Super Sports. Around 1932 the 3-speed model was introduced but the engines were changed from JAP to Matchless MX, MX2 and MX4 between 1933–35. Seen here (left and above) is a 1934 Super Sports fitted with a Matchless engine and a 3-speed with reverse gearbox.

its JAP engine tuned and the body re-styled, this subsequently became the Super Sports Aero.

Front brakes were an option by now, but these finally became standard in 1929 and two years later a new chassis accompanied a proper three-speed-and-reverse gearbox as well as a standard electric starter. The steel panels, wrapped around ash frames, did not change dramatically, but the three-wheelers did slowly take on a more modern look. There was even a delivery van for a few years.

Demand remained high enough to keep the factory busy and the designs were licensed as Darmont-Morgans in France. Some of the motor cycle V-twins used were water cooled and some air cooled, mostly from JAP or Matchless, and the three-wheelers were outstandingly successful, both on track and in trials.

The F-4, built between 1934 and 1952, was constructed on a totally new chassis and was restyled in 1935 and 1938.

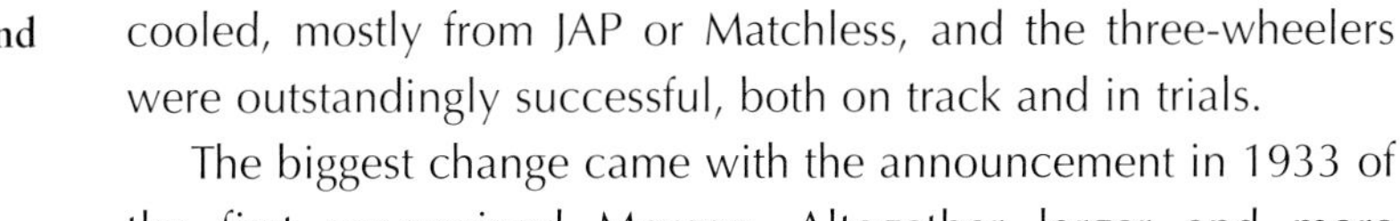

The biggest change came with the announcement in 1933 of the first car-engined Morgan. Altogether larger and more civilised, this had a 933cc four-cylinder Ford Model Y unit under its bonnet. For the first time, all its brakes were operated by the pedal and this was much more like a car with a wheel missing than a glorified cyclecar.

The major attraction of the Morgans had always been their low purchase price and low road tax (being classed as sidecar outfits), but after the Second World War purchase tax eroded the advantage. The V-twin models were dropped and it was left to the Ford cars, now with an 1172cc option, to carry the flag until 1952 when the company concentrated on its four-wheelers.

Featured here is the engine of the F4 – a radical change had taken place, the faithful V-twin having been replaced by a 4-cylinder, Ford, 10hp unit with 1172cc (71.51 cu in).

Morgan four-wheelers

Morgan is unique. Not only is this British company still owned by the family that founded it around 100 years ago, it continues to craft cars painstakingly by hand using traditional methods from those early days. And its order book remains healthy.

A fourth wheel was first added to a Morgan in 1936, when the 4/4 (four wheels, four cylinders) was displayed at the London and Paris motor shows of that year. The prototype shared its 939cc side-valve four-cylinder Ford engine with the newest of the three-wheelers for which the company was already famous and sat on a stretched version of that car's frame, but Morgans were expected to be fast and this one simply was not.

For production, a 1122cc, 38 bhp Coventry Climax engine, with overhead inlet valves, was substituted, together with a Meadows four-speed gearbox mounted remotely from the engine in the interests of even weight distribution. The steel convertible

The 4-4 was the first Morgan with four wheels. It appeared in 1936 and the official model designation 4-4 (later 4/4) stood for four wheels and four cylinders. Apart from a break during World War II and the period from March 1951 to September 1955, the 4/4 has been in continuous production, even up to 2009.

The original open two-seater 4-4 was the most popular of the three body options available. Featured here is a 1937 series 1 example.

Morgan 4/4
1945

Engine type	In-line four cylinder, ohv
Power	40 bhp @ 4300 rpm
Bore/stroke	63.5 x 100.0 mm (2.5 x 3.94 in)
Capacity	1267cc (77.3cu in)
Transmission	Rear drive, four gears
Wheelbase	2337 mm (92 in)
Top speed	128 kph (80 mph)

bodywork was wrapped round ash framing with room for just two seats. Morgan's patented sliding pillar front suspension was used, initially with lever-arm dampers, which also figured at the back, where a live axle was supported by semi-elliptic leaf springs. The drum brakes were cable operated and a worm-and-nut box looked after steering.

A four-seat version was quickly added and this was complemented in 1938 by a drop-head coupé which dispensed with the cut-away doors. There was also a new engine in this year: Standard made a special 40 bhp overhead-valve version of its side-valve 9 hp unit and this 1267cc four was paired with a Moss gearbox, still remotely mounted.

The 4/4 returned after the Second World War, but when Standard phased out the 1267cc engine it was replaced by the 68 bhp 2088cc Vanguard unit. The car had to be stretched a little to accommodate this and this was introduced as the Plus 4 in 1950. Standard's own gearbox was fitted, and hydraulic brakes appeared for the first time, together with telescopic front dampers. The top speed was now over 137 kph (85 mph).

The first significant alteration to the style of the cars was the introduction of a faired-in radiator cowl and grille, the curved shape covering the previously exposed flat radiator. In 1954, the

The instrumentation was comprehensive and near-to-hand for the driver.

A louvered bonnet and side-panels helped to disperse the heat from the engine compartment.

The early cars used a Coventry Climax engine, which was superseded from 1939 by a Standard Special 1267 cc (77.31 cu in) overhead valve engine. A four-speed Meadows gearbox was used until 1938, after which it was replaced by a Moss gearbox.

90 bhp, 1991cc Triumph TR2 engine was substituted, taking the top speed to more than 161 kph (100 mph). This was followed by TR3 and TR4 units.

A Super Sports version of the TR4-powered Series 4 car, with a tuned engine and lightweight body, could do over 185 kph (115 mph). A specially prepared version won its class at the Le Mans 24-hour race in 1962.

The 4/4 was not dead. The smaller model was re-introduced in 1955. Now powered by the 1172cc version of the old Ford side-valve engine, this was not fast, but at least it knocked 12 per cent or so off the Plus 4 price and there was a competition model, with a special cylinder head, for those who wanted it. As the Ford line-up changed, so too did Morgan's engines. Overhead valves arrived with the 997cc Anglia four, with a four-speed gearbox, and the capacity grew until the 1600 Cortina unit was fitted in 1963.

A big surprise for that year was the glassfibre-bodied Plus 4 Plus fixed-head coupé, based on the Plus 4 chassis and TR4-powered. It had mod-cons like winding windows, but it was a flop and only 25 of these were built in a two-year life.

In 1968, as the TR4 unit aged, Morgan shoe-horned Rover's 3.5-litre V8 into a longer and wider chassis and body, making the Plus 8. With 155 bhp, this gave 201 kph (125 mph) performance. Rover's gearbox ousted the Moss unit in 1972 and the 200 bhp Rover Vitesse engine gave even higher speeds in 1983, with standard rack-and-pinion steering.

Ford's 1.6-litre cross-flow engine went into the 4/4 in 1968 and continued to provide power until 1982, when the newer

This is an incredibly beautiful Morgan Plus 4 of 1993 (top) which has the Rover T16, single point injection engine fitted to it (right).

Morgan made good use of the new Triumph TR series engine in its Plus 4 model. The engine shown is the Triumph TR4, 2138 cc (130.5 cu in) of 1966 (above), which was used as the power unit for the Morgan Plus 4 of the same year (right).

From this angle the Plus 8 looks slim and fast. The leather strap across the bonnet makes sure the engine cover is safely locked down, whilst the slats on the bonnet disperse the heat from the big engine.

Part of the reason for the car being named the Plus 8 was due to the big Rover V8 engine that was fitted to the car.

Ford CVH, of similar capacity, took over. Along the way, a 1.6-litre Fiat twin-cam became an option and a 2-litre version of this powered the Plus 4 when it was re-launched in 1985.

Since then, with the occasional break, the four-cylinder models have continued in ever-improved but always traditional forms, using Ford and Rover power. In 2008 the 4/4 Sport had Ford's 1.6-litre Sigma engine, while the Plus 4 had the same company's 145 bhp 2-litre Duratec unit. The Plus 8 was dropped in 2004 and replaced by the Roadster, with a 225 bhp Mondeo 3-litre V6 and 216 kph (134 mph) a possibility.

Lightweight options have figured throughout the Morgan story and competition success in events from the RAC Rally to the Le Mans 24-hour race has been extensive. Remaining small has allowed Morgan not just to retain its traditional values but to build bespoke cars, either for road or for race track. One of the oldest manufacturers in the world, it had moved bang up to date as its centenary approached, not just with its superfast BMW V8-powered Aero 8, which finally had independent rear suspension and a wishbone front-end plus a new chassis and aluminium body, but with a hydrogen-powered "Life Car" concept.

Beautifully presented, this Plus 8 has aluminium wheels. Spoked wheels at this time were not recommended, as they couldn't deal with the power that the Morgan was capable of.

The wood veneer finish dashboard is just one of a selection of personal features that can be ordered. Each customer has a choice of interior and exterior equipment, allowing them to stamp their own character on the car.

Morris "Bullnose"

William Morris, later Lord Nuffield, was an Oxford motor agent when he decided in 1910 that there was scope to build a simple car with low running costs. He reckoned that a car like this would sell in large numbers, the British equivalent of the Model T Ford.

Rather than build every component himself, Morris bought parts in from outside suppliers and assembled his new car at a small factory in Cowley, just outside Oxford. The car was called the Morris Oxford. Announced in 1913, this was a two-seater, with a distinctive rounded radiator that earned it the nickname "Bullnose". The four-cylinder 1018cc engine came from White & Poppe, complete with a gearbox.

In March 1913 WRM Motors, a company set up by William Morris, produced its first car, the Morris Oxford (below). It was assembled rather than manufactured, by using components from many well-know firms of the period. The 9 hp engine, for example, was one produced by White & Poppe of Coventry, England (right).

Morris Oxford 1913

Engine type:	In-line, four-cylinder, sv
Power:	16.4 bhp
Bore/Stroke:	60 x 90 mm (2.36 x 3.54 in)
Capacity:	1018 cc (62.12 cu in)
Transmission:	Rear drive, three gears
Wheelbase:	2134 mm (85 in)
Top speed:	72 kph (45 mph)

These early cars were known as "Bullnose" models, quite simply because of the characteristic shape of the radiator at the front of the car. These were typical of pre First World War cars and found favour with much of the motoring population of the time.

A large and thick wooden steering wheel gave the driver good grip and better control of the vehicle.

What could be classed as the headlights, were of the acetylene type while the side and tail lamps were run on oil.

Morris was quickly proved right: this Oxford was a great success, but it was too small to have more than two seats. Unlike many manufacturers, Morris managed to continue production during the First World War and he introduced the Oxford's more famous successor, the Cowley, in 1915.

He had intended to use a new White & Poppe engine, but an exploratory trip to the United States had shown that he could buy engines and other components much more cheaply there. He opted for a 1495cc four from Continental of Detroit. This was a more modern unit altogether, with a detachable cylinder head (still with side valves) and a dynamo to provide electric lighting in place of the Oxford's combination of acetylene and oil lamps.

Not only was the Cowley bigger than the Oxford, with a choice of two- or four-seat bodywork, it was cheaper. As with the Oxford, there was a three-speed-and-reverse gearbox driving a surprisingly modern spiral-bevel rear axle through a torque tube. Three-quarter elliptic springs supported this, while the solid front axle relied on semi-elliptic items and there were no dampers

A single speedometer was sufficient instrumentation for the period and the mileage counters were also incorporated in a clear and precise fashion – not too dissimilar to today!

Found derelict in 1965 and restored by the current owner over a three year period from 1983, this 1923 Morris Cowley, two-seater plus dickey seat has beaded edge tyres and rear wheel brakes only. The car can be easily transformed into a convertible, the hood takes little time or effort to take down or put back up again.

Simple wooden dashboard with a good selection of dials and instruments were available to the driver.

until 1923. Braking was only on the rear wheels, but it was unusually effective.

The price might have been low, but corners had not been cut. There was leather upholstery and mahogany trim, plus nickel plating for many parts. Unfortunately new import restrictions conspired against the Cowley, both by pushing its price up through extra taxation and, in 1916, by banning all component imports unless they were for commercial use. Morris got round the last of these by introducing a van body.

Almost half of the 3000 engines ordered went to the bottom of the Atlantic during the war, a loss that made itself felt when peace returned. Continental no longer wished to build what was known as the Red Seal engine, but Morris owned the rights to it and had it made instead by Hotchkiss in Coventry.

The Smith, five-jet carburettor – straight through type (right), feeds the engine of the 1924 Morris Cowley (right). A Lucas GA4 magneto is also fitted as per all the 1925 and 1926 Oxfords and Cowleys. Detachable aluminium water outlet flange on the cylinder head was used up until December 1924 and the three-bladed, aluminium fan was used until April 1925.

The post-war Cowley had not changed significantly, except that it had been re-joined by an Oxford model. Both types now had a slightly bigger and more powerful engine and a shared chassis, but the Oxford was essentially a de luxe model. The Cowley now did without leather seats and full instrumentation and the Oxford was moved further up-market in 1920 with the introduction of an optional 2.3-litre six-cylinder version, made longer to accommodate that engine. Although this was listed until 1926, it was not popular.

A beautifully restored 1924 Morris Cowley, two-seater with dickey seat. Front-wheel brakes were fitted to this model.

Seen here is a 1926 Morris Cowley, four-seater Tourer. It had an 11.9-hp, 4-cylinder, 1550cc (94.6 cu in) side-valve engine fitted, with three forward and one reverse gear. Front-wheel brakes were fitted as standard to the Cowley range from the 1926 season and all brakes were rod operated.

Morris made a mistake when he increased the price of both models in the years immediately after the war, something that was not helped by a swingeing purchase tax. Sales plummeted at the end of 1920 and, realising his mistake, Morris cut 20 per cent off the four-seater's price and a little less off the two-seater's. This soon had the desired effect. And he did not stop there: just as his competitors were catching up he made a further 17 per cent reduction for the 1921 Motor Show. With their relatively small engines, the Bullnose Morrises had a substantial advantage over

The Morris Oxford Three-quarter coupé (below), was a new model produced in 1926 to meet the demand for an enclosed two-seater car, with easily accessible rear dickey seat that would accommodate two passengers. It has more than the usual refinements and a very comprehensive dashboard (above).

This 1926 Morris Oxford used a 13.9-hp engine and was available in a choice of four colours, Blue, Claret, Brown and Grey.

Affectionately known as the "Bullnose" Morris because of the shape of the radiator, production ceased in August of 1926.

The 1548cc engine of the 1926 Oxford was of Continental design, made by the British branch of the French Hotchkiss Company in Coventry.

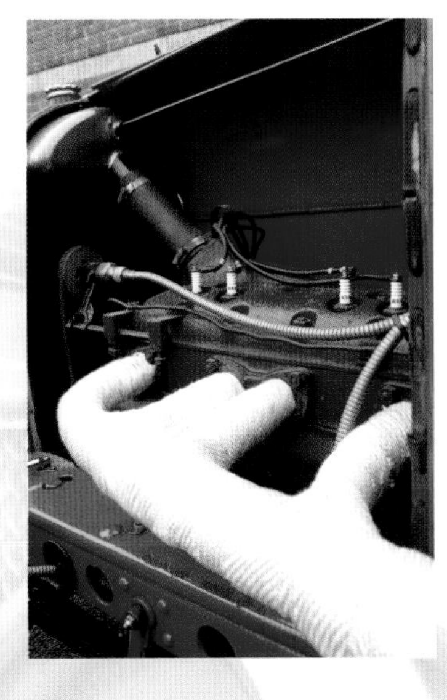

Seen here is the 4-cylinder, 1803 cc (110 cu in) engine of Red Flash, which competed at Brooklands in 1925. Driven by Cyril Paul, it never really made its mark, but is of interest as one of the many tuned-up, standard models which were very much part of the Brooklands scene at the time.

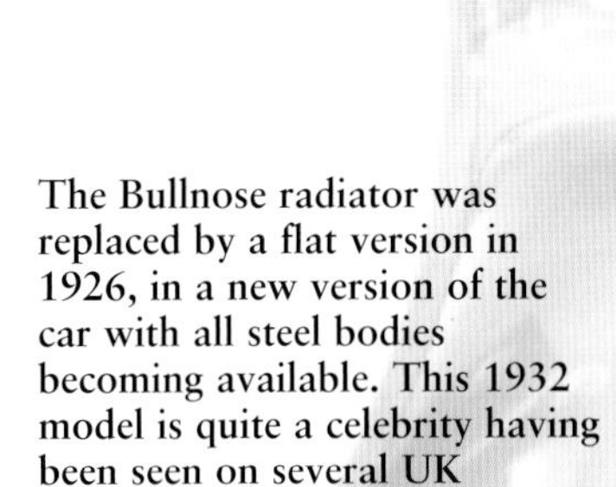

A Morris distributor in Wales by the name of HR Wellsteed, had this vehicle built in 1925 using a modified Morris Oxford chassis. The Red Flash was built with racing at Brooklands circuit near Weybridge in Surrey in mind. It managed a standing lap at over 125 kph (78 mph) and had a top speed of 128 kph (80 mph) plus.

the big-engined Model T because of the tax that was based on the RAC horsepower rating – which was itself based on engine capacity.

Specifications improved further over the next few years, but prices continued to come down. Morris took over the Hotchkiss engine plant in 1923 and increased the Red Seal's capacity to 1802cc. A run of 107 pretty aluminium-bodied sports cars had been produced by the factory in 1921–22 but different bodies were always available from coachbuilders – at a cost. Other improvements included a decent electric starter, balloon tyres and better instruments.

In 1926, rod-operated front brakes arrived, together with a new front axle that gave better steering response. However, with 154,000 cars built, sales declined dramatically and by the end of that year a new, flat-radiator model was in the showrooms.

The Bullnose radiator was replaced by a flat version in 1926, in a new version of the car with all steel bodies becoming available. This 1932 model is quite a celebrity having been seen on several UK television programmes.

Morris Minor

Sir Alec Issigonis has become synonymous with the BMC Mini, but his work was well known more than a decade before the Mini was launched. Yet to be knighted, he began his work for Morris in 1936 and designed the Morris Ten of 1939. During the Second World War, he was largely engaged on military projects, but he found time to toy with fresh ideas for cars – not least their suspension – and in 1944 he began work on a model on which he could put his ideas to the test.

He opted for a small and economical family car, going against the flow in believing that petrol rationing would stay in force for some years once peace returned. He was right. It was four years before his new Morris Minor appeared, but when it did it created something of a sensation, partly for its looks and partly because of its frugal fuel consumption.

From the start, Issigonis settled on unitary construction, which had already featured in his Morris Ten, and he added independent front suspension to the mix, with wishbones acting on torsion bar springs and lever-arm dampers providing the upper transverse links. He intended the torsion bar theme to

The prototype name of the Morris Minor was originally the Mosquito.

A significant design alteration that was made by Issigonis was to widen the car by four inches, which would give it enhanced stability and better road holding. The inside was pretty sparse but practical, made to reflect a price that would attract buyers from all walks of life. Post war life in England was hard and not everybody could afford a car, but they might be able to afford a Morris Minor – in fact it was the first British car to sell more than one million units.

extend to the rear, but in the event he had to make do with a live axle with semi-elliptic leaf springs.

The original plan was for a horizontally opposed water-cooled four-cylinder engine to be mounted forward in the chassis where it could possibly drive the front wheels. In the event, time constraints meant that it would not be possible to develop such a system. The Morris Eight side-valve in-line four was used and front-wheel drive would have to wait another decade or so for the Mini. With 918cc, the engine developed 27 bhp, which meant that it was quite efficient for the time.

A four-speed gearbox had synchromesh on the upper three ratios and was connected by a propeller shaft to a modern hypoid-bevel final drive. The gearchange left something to be desired, being of the "pudding stirrer" variety – a long and long-travel lever protruding from the floor. Rack-and-pinion steering was up to the minute, as were the hydraulically operated drum brakes on all four wheels.

The Minor was launched at the 1948 London Motor Show with a choice of two body styles, saloon or open tourer, both with two doors and four seats. The curved style clearly owed something to American fashion of the time, but it simply looked right – the more so since Issigonis had asked the development mechanics to cut a car down the middle and pull the sides apart, by 102 mm (4 in) as it happened, until he thought that the car looked right. With plenty of room for passengers and a reasonable amount of luggage, the Minor was easy to drive and could do a respectable 105 kph (65 mph). It was not surprising that it caught the public eye.

The early Morris Minors can be distinguished by the way the lights are fitted to either side of the grille. The first delivery to the US saw them fitted into the upper wings to meet safety regulations. This became the standard for all Minors in the UK in 1951.

Direction indicators were fitted but were positioned low on the side of the car, unlike most others of the period that had them higher on the side door pillar.

When production of the first series Morris Minor ended, just over a quarter of a million had been sold. It was a popular and reliable little car that reached the masses.

Morris Minor
1948

Engine type:	In-line, four-cylinder, SV
Power:	27.5 bhp @ 4400 rpm
Bore/stroke	57 x 90 mm (2.24 x 3.54 in)
Capacity:	918.6cc (56 cu in)
Transmission:	Rear drive, 4-gears
Wheelbase:	2184 mm (86 in)
Top speed:	102 kph (64 mph)

The Minor was originally designed to accept a flat-4 engine, with four distinctive gaps in the engine bay to accommodate it, but late in the development stage it was replaced by the 918.6 cc (56 cu in) unit.

One unusual aspect of the design was that the headlamps were mounted in the radiator grille in the early cars. Rumours that Europe was about to follow America's lead with minimum height requirements meant that by 1951 they had been incorporated into the front of the wings.

With the style set, the Minor was on its way, with booming sales. There were few major changes during its life, but one came in 1952 when, as a result of the merger with Austin to form the British Motor Corporation, the A30's overhead-valve A-series engine was dropped into the car. Although smaller than the side-valve unit, at 803cc, this gave 3 bhp extra and kept performance up to scratch.

The Morris Minor was again updated in 1956 when the engine was increased in capacity and the two-piece split windscreen was replaced with a curved one-piece one.

The Morris Minor was produced from 1948 through to 1971 and of all the types the convertible – or Tourer as it was correctly known – was probably the most desirable. It has a simple and easily recognisable shape but like most of the others, not a lot of performance, with its small capacity engine.

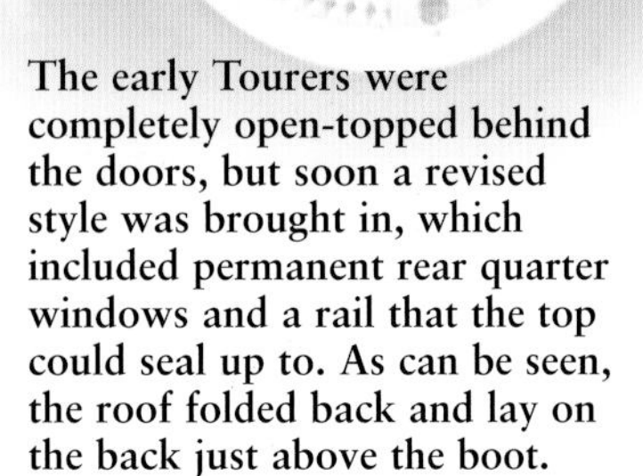

The early Tourers were completely open-topped behind the doors, but soon a revised style was brought in, which included permanent rear quarter windows and a rail that the top could seal up to. As can be seen, the roof folded back and lay on the back just above the boot.

According to the owner, not too much work had to be carried out to keep this superb Morris Minor Traveller in its original condition. Neither body panels nor wood had to be replaced.

Van, pick-up and wood-framed traveller versions were launched in 1953 and the next major change came when the engine was enlarged to 948cc in 1956. Top speed was now up to 113 kph (70 mph) and a remote gearchange improved the driving experience. An enlarged rear window was fitted at the same time as the distinctive split-windscreen was replaced by a curved one-piece item.

In 1961, when flashing indicators replaced the semaphore arms, the one millionth Morris Minor left the factory. This landmark was celebrated by the manufacture of 350 lilac-painted cars badges as Morris 1,000,000s for use by dealers in their publicity efforts. These were eventually sold to the public and were easily spotted with their quite unpleasant colour.

The last engine change was made in 1962. The capacity of the A-series was increased to 1098cc and with improved synchromesh added to the package the Minor was much more lively than before. Fuel consumption had increased, but shortages were in the past, so 30 mpg was acceptable.

When the Morris Minor was replaced in 1971 by the Marina, which used many of the old components including the engine, more than 1½ million had left the Cowley production line. Enthusiasts clamoured to tell BL, as the corporation had become, that they had made a mistake – in phasing out the Morris Minor – and perhaps they had.

Certainly a well looked after engine. This is the 1098 cc (67 cu in) powerplant fitted to this 1971 Traveller.

Although there aren't too many dials and knobs, the speedometer is large and clear sat neatly at the centre of the dashboard (left). The Morris "M" emblem is neatly embedded into the chrome bonnet handle (below).

A winner of many awards, this Traveller has only done 61,000 miles (97,600 km) since being bought new.

Riley RM

Riley was one of the earliest British manufacturers – hence its slogan "As old as the industry, as modern as the hour". Unfortunately, after building some fine saloon and sports cars, the company found itself in financial difficulties in the 1930s, with the result that it was acquired by William Morris and his Nuffield Organisation in 1938, just in time for war to put a stop to all motor manufacturing activities.

For the time being, the company's Coventry factory was retained and Victor Riley remained as Managing Director, which enabled the company to retain some autonomy when peace returned in 1945, although a move to Abingdon was on the cards. The pre-war models were abandoned and a single new saloon, the RMA, was quickly introduced in 1945.

With a fabric roof, over a metal mesh, and steel bodywork formed in the traditional style over ash framing, this stylish saloon combined familiar lines with new mechanical equipment. The RM was immediately being praised for its abilities, as well as its looks, not least because of the precise control that came from

The rarest of the RM variants, especially in Britain, was the RMC (below), a three-seater, two-door roadster version of the RMB introduced in 1948. The sleek lines were even more attractive once the roof was down and the windscreen could be folded flat too. Just behind the roof storage compartment, there was also a substantial area for luggage (left).

rack-and-pinion steering and independent front suspension by torsion bars and wishbones. This was carried on a sturdy steel chassis, as was the live rear axle, with leaf springs. There were telescopic dampers all round and the brakes combined mechanical and hydraulic operation at first, although there was an upgrade to full hydraulics in 1952.

One element that was carried over from the pre-war Rileys was the 1.5-litre four-cylinder engine. This was unusual in that it had twin camshafts mounted in its cylinder block, operating inclined valves in hemispherical combustion chambers, through pushrods and rockers. Its long stroke made it torquey and its 55 bhp was delivered at a relaxed 4500 rpm. The RMA made the most of this with a four-speed gearbox that had synchromesh on the upper three ratios.

Riley RMC 1949

Engine type	In-line four-cylinder, ohv with two camshafts
Power	100bhp @ 5500rpm
Bore/stroke	3.17 x 4.72in (80.5 x 120mm)
Capacity	149.1cu in (2443cc)
Transmission	Rear drive, four gears
Wheelbase	3023 mm (119 in)
Top speed	157 kph (98 mph)

In the front, there was a bench seat that could accommodate three people. The gearshift could be placed either on the steering column, mostly seen in the US and much more accommodating, or in the usual place in the middle of the floor just in front of the seat, as is shown here.

With the spare wheel carried on the rear of the car and the more compact interior meant that a larger boot could be included.

Late in 1946, the RMA was joined by the 2.5-litre RMB – in fact the models were known as the Riley 1½ and 2½ throughout the RM run. The RMB shared its construction with its sister car, and looked identical, but it was actually 7 inches longer to accommodate Riley's "Big Four". With a capacity of 2443cc, this had the same twin-cam arrangement as the smaller engine, but its bore and stroke dimensions were greater and with twin SU carburettors it developed 90 bhp at 4300 rpm to give the RME a top speed approaching 129 kph (80 mph).

Outside coachbuilders offered special bodies for the RMA, but drop-head versions of the RMB were made available by the factory. The RMC of 1948 was a roadster with cutaway doors,

The drivers accommodation (above) was spacious and comfortable and the instrumentation (left) was somewhat more sophisticated than the RMB. The RMC was intended for overseas markets, with most going to America, not surprisingly. Only 507 were constructed up until the end of the line in 1950.

aimed squarely at the American market. With three seats in a row, this had a column gear-change to make room for the passengers. The RMD, which arrived the following year, was a more conventional two-door convertible, with normal doors and four seats – and, as it turned out, was the last convertible to carry the Riley badge. By this time, the power of the Big Four engine had been boosted to 100 bhp, for the drop-heads as well as the standard RMB saloon, which could now manage over 145 kph (90 mph) and reach 97 kph (60 mph) in around 17 seconds. Unfortunately neither the home market nor the USA took to the convertibles and only 500 or so of each was built before these models were dropped in 1951.

The RMA was the first of the RM series of Riley cars, which were to be the last to be made independently by the company before being swallowed up by the ever-growing BMC organisation.

The instrumentation of the Riley RM series was somewhat different to other cars of the period and featured oblong shaped dials mixed with round main speedometer and tachometer dials, all on a neat wooden background.

The RMA used the 1.5-litre engine, which enabled the car to reach a respectable 121 kph (75 mph).

The frame of these cars was made of wood in the English tradition, and the car featured traditional styling to a high build standard. The RMA was produced between 1945 and 1952, when the RME came on the scene.

The RMA was updated in 1952. Apart from hydraulic brakes, what was now the RME had a new rear axle and propeller shaft and its rear window was enlarged. Further changes were made two years later when the running boards were removed and helmet shaped front wings with new headlamp fairings combined with spats that partly covered the rear wheels for a supposedly more streamlined look.

The interior was also given some attention. As the Riley press release of the time put it: "All upholstery is covered in the finest quality leather; a folding centre armrest is fitted to the rear seat and ash trays are readily to hand to drivers and passengers. A full set of instruments, including a water temperature gauge, ammeter and clock, are well grouped in a handsome walnut panel. A heater, with in-built demisting ducts, is fitted as standard".

By this time, the 2½-litre version had been replaced by the Pathfinder, which was coded RMH, but had a completely new full-width body, albeit with the Big Four engine. Nuffield had combined with Austin to form BMC in 1952 and the Pathfinder, of 1953 was the last real Riley.

Although the rear door of the RME and other RM series cars opened in what we would class as the correct way today, like many cars of that period, the front door opened the wrong way – that is to say that it is deemed unsafe to open a door that way. It wasn't long before all car doors opened the same way as the rear door, for safety reasons.

The RME (left and above) was an updated RMA and still used the faithful 1.5-litre, four-cylinder engine. In an attempt to increase acceleration a new rear axle was fitted with new gear ratios. The car featured a fully-hydraulic braking system and the rear window was made of curved glass and enlarged for better visibility (below).

The RMB had been updated in 1952, in the same way as the RMA, to become the RMF and in its 20-month life 1050 were built of what to many was the best of the series. It is said that the RME was due to be replaced by a smaller version of the Pathfinder, which might explain the lack of an RMG, but this never happened. The RME soldiered on until 1955, and was eventually replaced by the Riley 1.5, a BMC badge engineering job. Just under 9000 2½-litres and 14,000 1½s were built.

Rolls-Royce Silver Cloud

In the post-war Britain of 1945, Rolls-Royce, like other manufacturers, suffered from a shortage of materials, while high taxation and petrol rationing restricted the scope for luxury motor cars in the UK. Steel was more readily available for cars that were to be exported, so the Silver Dawn that was introduced in 1949 was aimed squarely at that market. Launched with left-hand drive, this was the first Rolls-Royce to have a standard steel body, since the specialist coachwork of previous cars imposed limitations on export potential.

Poor steel quality coupled with insufficient knowledge of, or attention to, corrosion protection prior to painting meant that the Silver Dawn was horribly rust-prone. However, Rolls-Royce designers were undeterred and they stuck to their new principles for the Silver Cloud that replaced the Dawn in 1955. Although by now most manufacturers had opted for unitary construction, in which the required overall rigidity was provided by a stressed body shell, the world's best-known car maker continued to fix its

When cars ran as smoothly as the Rolls-Royce, having a tray that would pull out was very handy, especially on long journeys.

The beautifully elegant Series I Silver Cloud. It oozed comfort and style and for anybody who wanted to be seen, this was the car to be seen in – Marilyn Monroe, Kiki Dee and Sir Elton John have all been linked to this particular car. It used an in-line, 6-cylinder engine and had a 4-speed automatic gearbox.

The Series II Silver Cloud was introduced in 1959, with minor changes to the exterior of the car. What did change was the engine which grew into a V8. It was now even heavier – hitting over 2-tons – but performance had also been enhanced with the new engine.

Little had changed at the front but the car was now fitted with power steering and there was the option of electric windows.

bodies to a separate chassis, albeit one that now benefited from the stiffness of welded rectangular-section members.

The standard body that cloaked this sturdy frame was an elegant creation styled by Chief Designer John Blatchley. Manufactured by Pressed Steel, it was every bit a Rolls-Royce and yet had been brought up to date, not least with proper full-width construction and large windows. The major constituents of the shell were steel, but the doors, the bonnet and the boot-lid were formed in aluminium. For the first time, the only differences between this and the Bentley equivalent, the S-type, lay in their radiators and their badges. There was not so much as an extra carburettor to boost performance.

Power was provided by an updated version of the straight-six of the previous models, with a new cylinder head. This had a capacity of 4887cc and had a combination of overhead inlet and side exhaust valves. Rolls-Royce engine output was always described as "adequate" and with twin SU carburettors, this unit, which was based on a previous military power plant, could

Rolls-Royce Silver Cloud II

1953

Engine type	V8, ohv
Power	Not quoted
Bore/stroke	104.1 x 91.4 mm (4.1 x 3.6 in)
Capacity	6223cc (379.8 cu in)
Transmission	Rear drive, four-speed automatic transmission
Wheelbase	3124 mm (123 in)
Top speed	166 kph (103 mph)

Pulling straight out from under the dashboard was a handy shelf, with ashtray. Instruments were clear, well presented and positioned right in front of the driver in a neat wooden panel.

propel the heavy Silver Cloud to 166 kph (103 mph). A four-speed automatic transmission was standard.

There was independent coil-spring suspension at the front, with an anti-roll bar, but the rear continued to rely on the earlier models' combination of a live rear axle and semi-elliptic leaf springs. There was a telescopic damper at each corner and those at the rear were electrically controlled. The cam-and-roller steering did not get power assistance, even as an option, until 1956. Rolls-Royce resisted the temptation to fit disc brakes throughout the life of the Silver Cloud, opting instead for a well-tried system of hydro-mechanically operated drums, with a gearbox-driven mechanical servo. Fortunately, this Royce had no sporting pretensions, otherwise its handling and braking might have been found seriously wanting.

Inside, the appointments were to the highest standard. Deep pile Wilton carpets, burr walnut veneer, soft and supple leather

This lady needs no introduction!

Two-tone paintwork sets the car off beautifully and anybody travelling in it would have felt special. Many of these cars were never driven by their owners; generally they would employ a chauffer.

Rear lights were a simple affair with brake and indicator set in one enclosure, with reflector built into the bottom of the assembly.

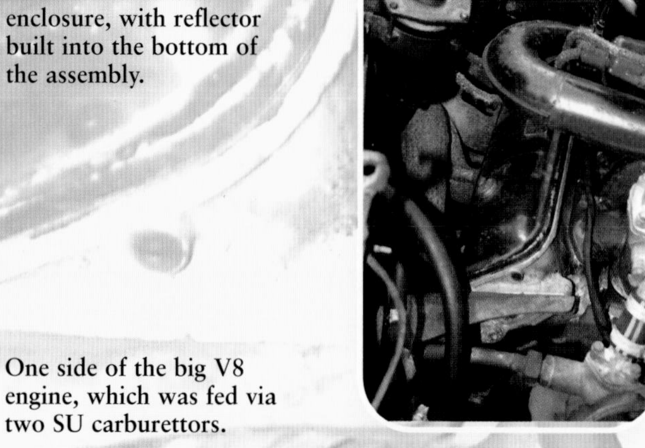

One side of the big V8 engine, which was fed via two SU carburettors.

upholstery and such niceties as armrests and picnic tables. Air conditioning was added to the list in 1956.

Unfortunately, the corrosion problems had not yet been overcome, but for those wanting something different it was still possible for rolling chassis to be supplied and for coach-built bodies to be added. There were also two wheelbase lengths to extend the possibilities.

By 1959, the modest performance of this 2-ton car was less acceptable, so Rolls-Royce fitted a brand new V8 engine. Still with pushrods, but now with all valves overhead, this aluminium

The convertible version of the Series II Silver Cloud was just magnificent. This one has been converted post purchase but you could order it direct from the factory. There was no lack of coachbuilders who would make this, or similar bodies for you.

The Series III Silver Cloud (below) did have slight differences to its predecessors. Immediately noticeable are the twin front lights and the much redesigned front wings (left). It lost some weight and the engine was tampered with to increase performance and top speed. This was the last of the series before making way for the forthcoming all-new Shadow.

unit had a 6.23-litre capacity. There was no longer an option to make manual gear changes. Top speed had gone up a little, but only to 169 kph (105 mph). According to a test in *The Motor*; the main improvement was in acceleration, which was now considerably faster.

Visually, the Silver Cloud II was almost identical to its predecessor. However, along with power steering came an option to have electrically operated side windows for the first time. The compact engine fitted without major modification to body or chassis and Rolls-Royce liked to stress that at 97 kph (60 mph) in a Cloud the loudest sound was that of the electric clock.

The final incarnation of the Silver Cloud was the S3. This arrived in 1963 and this time was clearly distinguishable. It had several minor body modifications, but twin headlamps on each side were instant identifiers. The interior had also been given a makeover. The mechanical essence of the model remained constant, but performance was boosted by a combination of reduced weight, larger carburettors and an increased compression ratio – the top speed was now up to over 185 kph (115 mph).

By now, it was an ill-kept secret that a new Rolls-Royce was under development. The four-headlamp Cloud III certainly paved the way for the similar frontal styling of the Silver Shadow that arrived in 1965, with unitary construction – and disc brakes at last. Silver Cloud production continued into 1966, by which time over 14,000 of those and the Bentley S equivalents had been made.

Rover P4

Known within the company as the first of the P4 series, the 75 was the first Rover in the modern post-war style. It might not have incorporated any leaps forward in mechanical sophistication, but it had an all-new full-width body that was steadily to evolve to keep the P4 in production for 15 years or so.

Rover's management had identified American Studebaker styling as showing the way ahead. Studebaker provided particular inspiration for the 75 concept, with its peculiar headlamp in the centre of the grille that not surprisingly earned

The original Rover P4, the model 75, arrived in 1949. It featured controversial modern styling which contrasted with its now outdated predecessor the P3. One particularly unusual feature was the centrally-mounted headlight in the grille, which led to the car being described as the "Cyclops". This was removed after 1952, when just the two outer lights were used.

Power for the 75 came from a 2.1-litre, Rover, IOE (inlet over exhaust) in-line, 6-cylinder engine, coupled to a four-speed manual transmission.

The early cars has a column-mounted gear change but this was changed to the floor-mounted unit from 1954. The instruments were oblong in shape and neatly arranged in front of the driver.

All P4s were seen as six-door saloons, with a three-person, comfortable bench seat at the front.

it the nickname "Cyclops". With all its corners rounded, the 75 was very distinctive when it was launched at the London Motor Show of 1949.

As modern as it looked, the 75's back doors were hinged at the rear in an arrangement that was fast falling out of favour, but one that was never to change throughout the P4 run. An ongoing post-war steel shortage meant that aluminium was used for the doors, bonnet and boot. Once inside, up to six people could be accommodated in comfort, with leather seats, plush carpets and plenty of solid wood trim.

The six-cylinder engine, with side inlet and overhead exhaust valves in an aluminium head, was carried over from the earlier P3 75, albeit now with twin SU carburettors and one or two other modifications. The capacity was 2103cc and the power output 75 bhp, hence the name. A four-speed gearbox, initially with

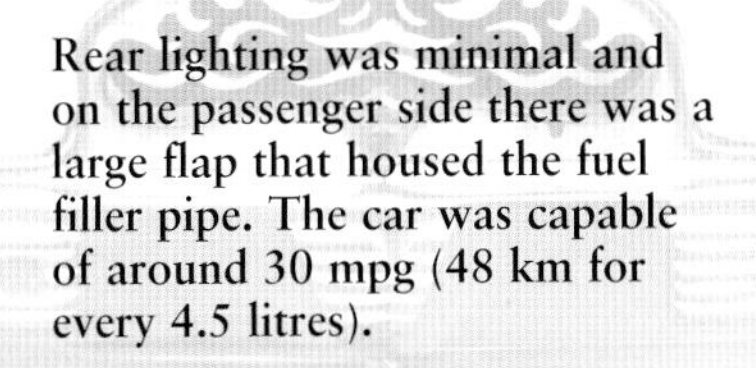

Rear lighting was minimal and on the passenger side there was a large flap that housed the fuel filler pipe. The car was capable of around 30 mpg (48 km for every 4.5 litres).

synchromesh only on third and top, had a column-mounted gear lever, to make way for a bench front seat, and a freewheel mechanism.

With a massive steel chassis, the 75 was quite a solid car, so its 134 kph (83 mph) top speed was not electrifying, although 0–100 kph (60 mph) in 21.6 seconds wasn't bad for the time. Passenger space had been made unusually large by pushing the front bulkhead, and thus the engine, well forwards. This gave a marked frontal weight bias which made the handling somewhat ponderous.

There was independent suspension at the front, with coil springs and wishbones, while the rear relied on a live axle, with semi-elliptic leaf springs and for a short time a Panhard rod. The worm-and-nut steering had no assistance and neither, at first, did the drum brakes, which had hydro-mechanical operation for the first year.

A P4 model 60 was introduced in 1953, but at the same time the top of the range model 90 (below) was also introduced, which had the more powerful six-cylinder engine. A single fog lamp was included so as to distinguish the 90 from its "lesser" stablemates, the 75 and 60 models. Front orange flashing indicators replaced the original white reflectors and "torpedo" style front sidelights (right) were also included.

Rover 90

The central headlamp was dropped in 1952 and for 1954 there were two additional P4 models. The 60 had a much-altered four-cylinder version of the 75 engine, shared with the Land-Rover, with its bores repositioned and enlarged and its stroke shortened, resulting in a capacity of 1997cc and, with a single carburettor, a 60 bhp output. Top speed was 122 kph (76 mph). The 90 borrowed the new cylinder arrangement, but retained the additional two bores, so that it had a 2638 cc (161 cu in) capacity and a 90 bhp on tap for a 149 kph (90 mph) maximum. While the 90 was seen as a worthwhile addition, the 60 was not a great success, being judged to be a significantly lesser car for only a slightly lesser price.

Styling revisions came in late 1954. A wrap-around three-piece rear window improved visibility, while the slope of the tail was made less steep and this added considerably to the boot space. The following year saw the 75's engine swapped for a short-stroke version of the 90 unit with its rearranged bores. The swept volume was now 2230cc and with just one carburettor the power output was a modestly more muscular 80 bhp.

Overdrive became an option in 1956, as did servo-assistance for the brakes of the 90. The freewheel was deleted if the servo was chosen, apparently to give engine braking should the servo system fail.

A view of one side of the big 6-cylinder engine from the Rover 90, showing the plugs, distributor, coil and oil filler cap. The black, torpedo looking thing in the background is the air filter.

Rover 90
1954

Engine type	In-line 6-cylinder, overhead inlet, side exhaust valves
Power	90 bhp @ 4500 rpm
Bore/stroke	73.03 x 105.0 mm (2.88 x 4.13 in)
Capacity	2638 cc (161 cu in)
Transmission	Rear drive, four gears
Wheelbase	2819 mm (111 in)
Top speed	149 kph (90 mph)

The Rover 90 has subtle changes to the bodywork that will distinguish it from the 100 model. The front wings have a different profile and immediately noticeable is the heavily sloping rear.

The column gearshift had gone and a long, cranked gear lever now took its place. The rather clumsy long handbrake, which was positioned at the right of the driver, was now replaced by a neat pull-up "shepherds crook" style handbrake, positioned at the side of the drivers seat, allowing better access and exit from the car.

The 100 version of the P4 was introduced in 1959 and like its predecessors had a steel bodyshell and Brimabright aluminium alloy doors and boot lid.

The front turn and park lights were now beautifully housed within the top of the wings, which had been reshaped to give a more modern and aerodynamic feel to the car.

Rover 100

An ill-starred "Roverdrive" automatic gearbox appeared for the first time in the 105R of late 1956. With minor exterior and trim amendments, this had a new twin-carburettor head on the 90 engine and developed 108 bhp. With just two normal ratios and an inefficient combination of fluid coupling and vacuum-operated clutch, the gearbox rendered the R's performance lifeless. Fortunately there was a manual equivalent, the 105S, now with overdrive as standard, which could manage the best part of 161 kph (100 mph) and get there far quicker than the automatic.

The automatic pain was short-lived, the R being withdrawn in 1958, followed by the S a year later, when the 60, 75 and 90 were also replaced by the 80 and 100. The 80 had a petrol version of the latest four-cylinder ohv Land-Rover diesel engine, with 77 bhp and a 137 kph (85 mph) capability – a better proposition than the 60. The 100 was blessed with a short-stroke adaptation of the six from the new 3-litre model, with seven instead of the previous four crankshaft bearings. Still with side inlet valves, this 2625cc (160.2 cu in) unit had 104 bhp to drive the 100 towards a still quite modest 153 kph (95 mph).

An air intake vent (above) positioned just in front of the windscreen, which was operated via a lever inside the cab. The beautiful, chromed, dished hubcaps were given a Rover badge, which was placed in an indent in their middle (right). With both doors open its easy to see that there is plenty of room in the car for six people, comfortably (below).

The 100 model had a large and spacious boot area which made this car ideal for long-distance touring.

A view of the 6-cylinder, 2625cc (160.2 cu in) engine, which had a cast iron block, alloy head and seven bearing crankshaft. With a top speed of 92.1 mph (147.4 kph) and a fuel consumption of 20.6 mpg (33 km for every 4.5 litres), it was neither fast nor frugal, but made up for those failings with its sheer luxury and comfort.

Both types now had front disc brakes, with standard servo assistance. Overdrive was also fitted to all cars.

The final variations on the P4 theme came in 1962 as stop-gaps when development of the P6 Rover 2000 was delayed. The 95 took over from the 80, now with a slightly detuned version of the 100 engine. The 110 had the same unit, but with a Weslake cylinder head and 123 bhp, making this the fastest of the P4s, finally scraping to the magic "ton" (161 kph). The 95 now made do without overdrive, but had a raised final drive ratio to compensate, although doing away with the aluminium panels towards the end can't have helped the performance.

P4 production finally came to an end in May 1964. More than 130,000 examples of one of the best-loved Rovers had been made.

SS90 & 100

When William Lyons moved from building his Swallow Sidecars to assembling cars, his beautifully crafted special-bodied Swallow Austin Sevens of 1927 created quite a stir. Encouraged by the public reaction, he moved his business from Blackpool to Coventry in 1928 and five years later began manufacturing complete cars sporting a new SS badge.

Lyons never made clear what the SS stood for, perhaps Standard Swallow or Swallow Special – or simply the initials of Swallow Sidecars – but SS Cars was formed as a Swallow subsidiary in 1933 and floated as a public company in its own right two years later. By this time, Lyons had done a deal with John Black of Standard, whose cars Swallow had also rebodied,

The SS90 of 1935 was Lyons' first true sports car, and took this title in anticipation of 90 mph (144 kph) being the achieved top speed. The model's chassis was essentially that of the revised SS1 with an underslung rear and 15 inches (381 mm) extracted from its central section. The really significant aspect of the 90 was the bodywork, which was very low with wide stylish wings and a very exposed cockpit (right).

to buy a special version of the company's six-cylinder engine. This he fitted into his first proper motor car, the elegant SS1 coupé.

The SS1, which was later available in saloon and tourer forms, certainly looked the part, and was the star of the 1931 London Motor Show. However, it was not as good as it looked and despite promising sales it was substantially altered a year later, most importantly with a longer, stiffer chassis. It was this frame that ultimately formed the basis of the new SS sports car, the SS90, which made its debut in March 1935.

That was the year in which Lyons's Swallow partner, William Walmsley, left the company, although it was he who had floated the idea of building a two-seater on a shortened chassis, albeit for his own enjoyment. The third of these SS1 two-seaters became the prototype for the SS90. Its frame was shortened by 381 mm (15 in) and clothed in a low and fast-looking convertible sports body, fashioned from aluminium panels formed round ash frames. Power was provided by the 2.7-litre Standard straight-six. Still with side valves at this stage, it had an SS aluminium cylinder head and some other modifications and produced around 70 bhp, which was sufficient for a top speed of roughly 145 kph (90 mph). A four-speed gearbox had synchromesh on all but first and reverse gears. Semi-elliptic leaf springs looked after suspension at both ends, with solid axles and lever-arm dampers. There was a cam-and-lever steering box and cable-operated four-wheel drum brakes.

Lyons was never one to stand still and he felt that his sports car deserved more power. He considered a number of options, including supercharging, but in the event turned to cylinder head specialist Harry Weslake to craft a new overhead-valve head for the Standard engine. Weslake worked quickly and by May 1935

SS Jaguar 90
1935

Engine type:	In-line, six-cylinder, sv
Power:	75 bhp
Bore/stroke	73 x 106 mm (2.87 x 4.17 in)
Capacity:	2663 cc (162.5 cu in)
Transmission:	Rear drive, 4-gears
Wheelbase:	2641.6 mm (104 in)
Top speed:	145 kph (90 mph)

Several controls were fitted to the centrepiece of the steering wheel – for example the lights and their various positions, along with the horn and direction indicators.

Handbrake and gear-lever were neatly positioned slightly under the dashboard but were easily accessible.

Although the prototype had covered spare wheel and built-in fuel tank, all production cars featured an exposed tank and wheel. The original design could probably have been discarded due to cost factors.

A view of the straight, 6-cylinder engine and its two RAG carburettors.

The SS100 model was not produced after the war, but a lone example had been stored away, unregistered throughout the war. Known by its subsequent registration, LNW 100, the car was very successful in the Alpine and Tulip Rallies in the hands of Ian Appleyard.

The front brakes on this car had a special intake channel which would filter the air directly to the brake drum, although a mesh was placed over the front to stop any dirt or stones from entering the system.

This was the last SS100 and although it started out with the 2½-litre engine it was replaced with the larger engine before being sold to Ian Appleyard to go racing with.

a prototype was producing over 100 bhp. With remarkable speed, new Chief Engineer William Heynes designed a new chassis and running gear to take this engine and the car was launched, along with a revised version of the SS90, at the October Motor Show. However, only 24 model 90s were ever produced.

For his new range, Lyons had chosen an equally new model name, Jaguar. This was selected from a list of animal names presented to him because of associations with a similarly titled First World War aero engine. The company did not become Jaguar Cars until 1945, with SS having gained unfortunate connotations, although the 90's replacement was now the SS Jaguar 100.

The bodywork was mildly revised, principally in a slight softening of the wing line and a more pronounced inclination to the rear panel and spare wheel. The suspension and steering were also uprated in detail, and the brakes were now rod operated. The car, though, was only six months old, so major changes, other than in the engine, were not to be expected.

The top speed was now up to 153 kph (95 mph), but the raised gearing restricted performance in exchange for a more relaxed

journey. As with the 90, the windscreen could be folded to reduce drag, but small aero screens could now be used instead to give occupants some protection.

As with Jaguars after the war, the SS Jaguars were notable for their low price. The sports cars were more expensive than cars such as MG Midgets, but they were considerably cheaper than more realistic competitors such as Aston Martins, the price of an SS100 being £395.

One further change was to come in the short life of the 100. In late 1937, a 3.5-litre version was introduced alongside the original. The enlargement had been achieved by siamesing the cylinders and increasing their diameters as well as the crankshaft stroke. Gearing was raised again and the 100 finally lived up to its name, reaching 162.7 kph (101.1 mph) in the hands of *The Motor* magazine's testers.

One more SS Jaguar 100 was to come. On the Motor Show stand of 1938, a Bugatti-style fixed-head coupé was exhibited. At a price of £595 it was the most expensive SS yet and it clearly attracted no real interest, that exhibit being the only example ever built. The standard two-seaters, despite their attractive looks and capable performance, never sold in quantity. Production continued into the war, but by 1940, when the last 100 left the Coventry works, only 314 had been made, 49 of which had gone abroad.

These emblems and badges (right and below) tell a little bit of history. When the SS (Swallow Sidecars) company moved to Coventry, they weren't known as Jaguar, which only happened after the war in 1945. This 3½-litre car though, was hidden until after the war.

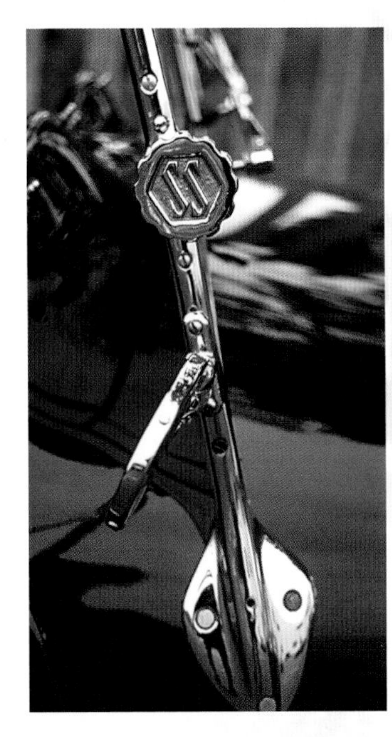

From a total of 314 produced, the less expensive 2½-litre cars made up the bulk of production with 198 being produced, compared with 116 of the more expensive 3½-litre cars, although the smaller capacity engine had been in production for longer than its larger stablemate.

Sunbeam-Talbot 80 & 90 & Sunbeam Alpine

Talbot is a name that has had several motor industry incarnations. When the Rootes Group took over the remnants of Sunbeam-Talbot-Darracq in 1935, it quickly dropped all but the Talbot badge. Sunbeam, it seemed, was dead. A new range of Talbot models, based around existing Rootes parts, was concocted and put on sale, but now unrelated Talbot-Lagos were being sold in France and this gave rise to unwelcome confusion. The Sunbeam name was revived in 1938, when existing Talbots were badged as Sunbeam-Talbots. A projected new flagship, the Sunbeam 30, was shown in prototype form at the Motor Show in October, although this was never to be produced.

The Sunbeam-Talbot 80 and Sunbeam-Talbot 90 were introduced in the summer of 1948. They had new streamlined bodywork and flowing front wings. The 80 (right and below) used the Hillman Minx based engine whilst the 90 had a modified version of the Humber Hawk engine. The 80 turned out to be very underpowered and was dropped just two years later in 1950.

When the Second World War ended in 1945, a couple of the old Sunbeam-Talbots, the 10 and the 2-litre, went back into production, but they had been based on earlier models when they were first launched, so something new was needed. What came in 1948 certainly looked very different from anything before, even if there were plenty of reminders beneath the skin.

The Sunbeam-Talbot 80 and 90 were built around the 2-litre's chassis and they retained not just a live rear axle, albeit widened a little, but beam front suspension, with semi-elliptic leaf springs all round. There was also worm-and-nut steering and, for the first time, hydraulically operated brakes. Gone were the fabricated metal panels on ash frames, replaced by new full-width pressed-steel bodies in four-door saloon and two-door drop-head coupé forms (the rear-hinged back doors were unusual in that they had no pillars between them and the quarter-lights).

It was the engines that distinguished the two cars. The 80's was an in-line four borrowed from the Hillman Minx but with its side valves ousted by overhead items. For the time, a power output of 47 bhp from 1185cc was not bad and there was a four-speed gearbox, with synchromesh on the upper three ratios and a column change, to make the most of this. Yet it really wasn't enough. The 80 weighed more than a ton, which meant that it took quite a while to struggle to its top speed of 117 kph (73 mph).

The 90, by contrast, could make 129 kph (80 mph) and reach 100 kph (60 mph) in 26 seconds, compared with the 80's 36, thanks to a similarly converted 1944cc four from the Sunbeam-Talbot 2-litre and Humber Hawk. This generated 64 bhp and gave a more relaxed ride through a higher final-drive ratio.

The Sunbeam Alpine, which appeared in 1953 was given its name due to the successes attained by the saloon models in the Alpine Rally in the early 1950s. The one seen here is an ex-works car used by a young Stirling Moss who, along with co-pilot John Cutts, raced the car quite successfully in the Rallye international des Alpes, both in 1953 and the following year.

This is the dashboard of the Alpine that was raced by Moss, not a standard layout – the tachometer is wrong – for the year but could well have been modified by the factory for racing.

The Alpine M I was also made in a "special" version in which the engine power was increased to 97.5 bhp, which enabled the car to reach over 160 kph (100 mph). The rally car featured, originally a "special", was further enhanced for racing – having larger fuel tank, bigger brakes, extra-light engine components to name but a few.

The doors on the 1955 Sunbeam MkIII were the type that opened in opposite way, thus allowing better access to the car. Interior trim was a mix of vinyls and leather finishes.

The current owner of this beautiful MkIII bought this car with only 3401 miles on the clock. Restoration was minimal – a professional respray was carried out due to lacklustre paintwork – with little being done to trim or mechanics even though it was nearly thirty years old. The colour is officially known as Alpine Mist.

Despite its lack of muscle and a not substantially advantageous price, the 80 sold almost as well as the 90, but its days were numbered. In 1950, a completely new chassis was added to the familiar body, but there was no 80 version of what was now the MkII. Independent front suspension had arrived, with coil springs, wishbones and an anti-roll bar, while the rear now had a Panhard rod for better location, and recirculating-ball steering was fitted. At the same time, the engine was bored out to 2267cc to deliver 70 bhp and, with raised gearing in a new back axle, a top speed of 138 kph (86 mph).

The styling was hardly changed. The front wings were modified to raise the headlamps by 76 mm (3 in) to please the American law-makers, while extra front air intakes replaced the fog and spot lamps.

In 1952 a MkIIA 90 improved on this again, largely through experience gained in very successful rally exploits. The power output was boosted a little, to 77 bhp, and this time the brakes were enlarged to match the performance. At the same time, the spats that had covered the rear wheels were removed to improve brake cooling.

The final 90 of 1954 dropped the Talbot part of the name and became simply the Sunbeam MkIII. The frontal styling was mildly revised, with some new adornments, and there was a new dashboard, with an optional rev counter. Another 3 bhp was squeezed from the engine, which could now be had with overdrive, and the MkIII could manage 152 kph (94 mph).

In addition to the saloon and four-seat drop-head, Rootes introduced an elegant two-seat sporting convertible in 1953, which was called the Alpine after a rally in which the 90s had done very well. It was based on a one-off made by Bournemouth dealer George Hartwell and it shared its basic mechanical components (80 bhp engine) with the 90, although its chassis was stiffened, as was the suspension, and there was more direct steering.

Only seen on the MkIII, these are air vents for the engine compartment.

A most elegant looking car that was seen as an up-market model in 1955. It's probably quite difficult to understand today, but the front seats could be removed at the click of a button. This was so that if you wanted to stop on the side of the road to have a picnic, you could use the seats to sit on!

Sunbeam MKIII 1955

Engine type:	In-line, four cylinder, OHV
Power	80bhp @ 4400 rpm
Bore/stroke	81 x 110mm (3.2 x 4.3 in)
Capacity	2267 cc (138.4 cu in)
Transmission	Rear drive, 4 gears
Wheelbase	2477 mm (97.5 in)
Top speed	150 kph (93.6 mph)

The Sunbeam had a column gearchange, which wasn't uncommon at the time. The gears were all fitted with synchromesh except first and reverse. Again quite normal for the time.

The MkIII Alpine used an 80-bhp, four-cylinder engine and overdrive transmission was now standard equipment. Sunbeam Alpines were much sought-after performance cars and they enjoyed racing success in the UK and abroad.

The car still has the original C-41 Dunlop tyres and the spare wheel and tyre have never been used.

The body was instantly recognisable as part of the 90 family, but having only two seats it had gained a long, flowing tail. Aimed at the American market, the Alpine was initially built only in left-hand-drive form, but home market editions were soon available. As with the saloon, overdrive was offered in 1954 and the sports car could climb to a top speed of 153 kph (95 mph).

Despite emulating the 90's sporting success, the Alpine was not a big seller. Some 3000 were sold before the model was withdrawn in 1955. The MkIII went on for another two years, by which time more than 25,000 80s and 90s had been built.

Triumph TR2–7

The range that set Triumph up as one of Britain's best-known sports car builders had a very shaky start. Standard had bought what remained of the ruined company in 1944. In the hard times that followed the war, Standard Chairman Sir John Black identified an opportunity to produce a new sports car for the American market, where companies such as MG and Jaguar were highly successful. The trouble was, he was in a hurry and he did not want to spend much money.

Having had his offer to buy Morgan politely refused, Black set his own people to work on the sports car that he had in mind. Mindful of the cost constraints, the head of the styling department Walter Belgrove and chassis engineer Harry Webster used as many off-the-shelf Standard parts as they could. With only a meagre £16,000 at his disposal to tool up for body production, Belgrove had to opt for the unsuitably flimsy chassis from the pre-war Standard Flying Nine. This was equipped with the independent coil spring front suspension and live rear axle from the Triumph Mayflower saloon, and the whole effort was

A Triumph TR2 seen in a typical rural English scene. This model was built between 1953 and 1955 by the Standard Motor Company, England. The body was mounted on a separate chassis; it had coil-sprung independent suspension at the front and a leaf spring live axle at the rear. You could chose from wire or disc wheels and it had a 4-speed manual gearbox unit with overdrive available on top gear as an option. Drum brakes were fitted all round.

Seen here is a Triumph TR3A, which was basically an uprated version of the TR3. The changes included a new wide front grille, exterior door handles, lockable boot handle and it now came with a full tool kit as standard.

The TR2 used a twin SU carburettor version of the 1991 cc (121.5 cu in) four-cylinder Standard Vanguard engine, tuned to increase its output to 90 bhp.

Triumph were famous for having their headlights in this style. No wonder the Sprite got the nickname "frogeye".

The interior of this car has recently been restored. Instrumentation was comprehensive and clear to read for the driver.

driven by a small-bore 1991cc version of the Standard Vanguard engine, albeit with twin carburettors and a four-speed gearbox.

With a shape closely resembling that of the eventual TR2, a prototype, the 20TS (never officially known as the TR1), was displayed at the 1952 London Motor Show. It had a projected price of £555 plus purchase tax, but fortunately before any cars were built for sale the show model was entrusted to respected test driver and mechanic Ken Richardson, to elicit his opinion on the design. He cut his test drive short, so much did he dislike the Triumph, and declared it a death trap.

Rather than consign the project to an early grave, Black took Richardson on to develop the new sports car into what it should have been. Within three months this had been achieved by the team and in March 1953 the Geneva Motor Show audience caught the first glimpse of what was now the TR2.

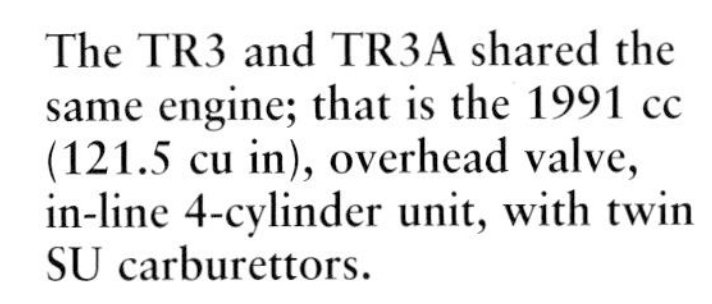

The TR3 and TR3A shared the same engine; that is the 1991 cc (121.5 cu in), overhead valve, in-line 4-cylinder unit, with twin SU carburettors.

The TR4 made its debut in 1961 and was based on the chassis and drivetrain of the previous TR sports cars. The new modern body style was by Italian design house Michelotti.

The box-section chassis was new and the rear of the body that it carried had been re-designed to house the previously external spare wheel. The power output of that pushrod four-cylinder engine had gone up from 75 to 90 bhp, and when *The Motor* magazine carried out a road test it achieved a top speed of 172 kph (107 mph).

Priced slightly above the old-fashioned MG Midget and considerably below the new Austin Healey 100, the TR2 was soon selling well. It also quickly proved itself in competition, winning the RAC Rally of 1953 in private hands. It had its foibles, as contemporary road tests pointed out, not least a tendency for the back to try and overtake the front on hard cornering, but it was reliable, fast and – with 30 mpg fuel consumption – remarkably economical.

By the time the TR3 arrived in 1955, Triumph was already listing overdrive and wire wheels as options, along with the heater that was usually specified. The new model had a distinctive grille in what had been simply a hole in the nose and the engine had been mildly tuned to push out another 5 bhp. It was to be another year or so before front disc brakes were fitted, replacing the less than perfect drums. Most cars were two-seaters, but a small bench rear seat was an option, as was a good quality steel hardtop.

Further tuning, to 100 bhp, was introduced before the TR3A appeared in 1958. The grille was now full width and the doors and boot were lockable, although locking the doors of a convertible is of dubious benefit. In what was noted as a reliable car, it was perhaps strange that the previously optional tool kit was made standard equipment.

Although the TR3A continued to sell well, with the vast majority of cars going abroad, it was clear that something new would soon be needed. Triumph was very active in the Le Mans

Although the engine from the TR2/TR3 models continued to be used, the displacement was increased to 2138cc (130.5 cu in) in the TR4 by using a larger diameter piston.

No mistaking that grille anywhere, although the "frogeye" style lights had now been replaced.

The Triumph TR5 was built for 13 months – between August 1967 and September 1968. It was basically the same as the Michelotti styled TR4 with the main differences hiding under the bonnet.

24-hour race at this time, and the new twin-overhead-camshaft engine that was used – eventually to take the team prize – was originally destined for the new road car. With company finances beginning to falter, this car had several false starts, but with the twin-cam side-lined the TR4 was built on what was essentially the TR3A chassis, with widened track and rack-and-pinion steering.

The old three-bearing engine was retained and bored out to 2138cc to produce 105 bhp. With an all-synchromesh gearbox (overdrive remained an option), this roadster, with its stylish new body from the pen of Italian specialist Michelotti, could manage 175 kph (109 mph). That body was wider, longer and lighter than the TR3's, and it provided more room for the passengers including children in the back. A hard-top with a removable metal roof panel was an option, the panel later being replaced by fabric in a Surrey top arrangement. Wind-up windows and face-level ventilation completed the package.

This was launched in 1961, but thanks to reservations about it from across the Atlantic a modified TR3, known as the TR3B, was sold in the USA for a further year, with the new gearbox and a choice of 2-litre or 2.2-litre engines.

The most important differences between the TR5 (left) and its predecessor was that it used a 2.5-litre, in-line 6-cylinder, fuel injected engine, which could produce 150 bhp. At this time, fuel injection (or petrol injection as it was called) in road cars was new and Triumph let it be known, through their sales brochure, that the TR5 was the "First British production sports car with petrol injection".

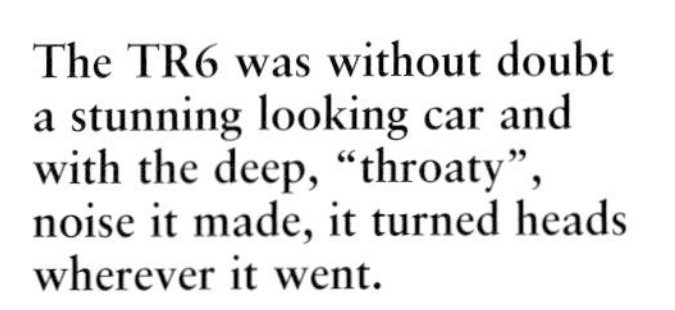

The TR6 was without doubt a stunning looking car and with the deep, "throaty", noise it made, it turned heads wherever it went.

All TR6 sports cars featured the in-line, 6-cylinder engines. The engine for the US export model had carburettors, while all other export markets, including England, used a fuel injected version, as seen here.

The TR6 had independent rear suspension, rack and pinion steering, 15-inch (381 mm) wheels and tyres and bucket seats. The front brakes were disc and the rear were drums.

America soon grew to love the TR4, and sales escalated there in 1962. However, more comfort was sought. The answer lay in independent rear suspension added to a revised chassis and using semi-trailing arms and coil springs with lever-arm dampers. Introduced in 1965, this gave a much better ride, but just in case the American market resisted the change, a new live axle set-up was an option on what was now the TR4A. Other changes to the car were largely cosmetic, but now the search was on for more power.

The old four-cylinder engine was really past its best. After considerable development a long-stroke 2498cc version of the Triumph 2000 saloon's 2-litre ohv six was shoe-horned into the old chassis, using the original transmission. The most notable development was the installation of Lucas fuel injection that pushed the power output up to 150 bhp and made this new TR5 of 1967 capable of 188 kph (117 mph). Paradoxically, the US market, with its strict emission regulations, had to make do with carburettors and only around 110 bhp in what was called the TR250.

The TR5 was pretty well identical to the TR4A in looks and other mechanical details. Inside it featured several cosmetic and safety-related improvements and a new folding hood finally did away with any space behind the seats for an occasional seat.

Instrumentation was clear and easy to read, whilst "rocker" style switches were used for lights and other accessories.

Triumph TR6
1969

Engine type	In-line six cylinder, ohv
Power	150 bhp @ 5500 rpm
Bore/stroke	74.7 x 95.0 mm (2.94 x 3.74 in)
Capacity	2498cc (152.4 cu in)
Transmission	Rear drive, four gears
Wheelbase	2235 mm (88 in)
Top speed	188 kph (117 mph)

Power for the TR7 came via a 1998 cc (122 cu in), 8-valve 4-cylinder engine, which was mounted in-line at the front of the car. Drive was to the rear wheels via a four-speed gearbox initially, with optional five-speed gearbox or three-speed automatic from 1976.

The TR7 was launched in the US in January 1975 and before the home market, which saw its launch in May 1976. Even then it was after some delays due to the high demand in the US. Originally a hardtop, the convertible did finally follow and added to the record-breaking sales.

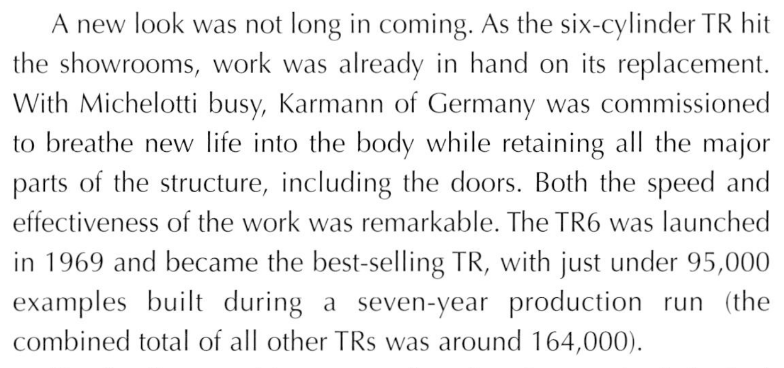

A new look was not long in coming. As the six-cylinder TR hit the showrooms, work was already in hand on its replacement. With Michelotti busy, Karmann of Germany was commissioned to breathe new life into the body while retaining all the major parts of the structure, including the doors. Both the speed and effectiveness of the work was remarkable. The TR6 was launched in 1969 and became the best-selling TR, with just under 95,000 examples built during a seven-year production run (the combined total of all other TRs was around 164,000).

The family resemblance was clear, but the new body looked very modern and the top speed was similar to that of the TR5. In 1973, the engine was slightly detuned in the interests of improved driveability, but the TR6 remained popular until it was replaced by the TR7, which had unitary construction and shared no common parts.

The TR7 was characterised by its "wedge" shape, which the company advertised as "The Shape of Things to Come". This design was created by Harris Mann who had also designed the wedge-shaped Leyland Princess. Pop-up front lights added to the cars appeal (left).

TVR S

The history of TVR is famously chequered. Established by Trevor Wilkinson (TVR was a contraction of his first name) in 1947, the Blackpool-based company had been through several financial wobbles by the time it was purchased by Peter Wheeler in 1982. During the first couple of years of his stewardship several new models were introduced, largely based on earlier types, but he believed that there was room in the market for a traditional sports car that could be made in greater quantities to fill the gap once occupied by the likes of the MGB, the TRs and the big Healeys.

Wheeler's plan came to fruition at the London Motor Show of 1986, where the TVR S made its debut. This bore a strong

Featured here (left) is the big 3948cc (241 cu in), Rover V8 powerplant for this 1992 TVR S (below). With a 0 to 96 kph (60 mph) time of 4.9 seconds and a top speed of 238.4 kph (149 mph) this was no slouch. 2604 "S" models were made between 1986 and 1994, of which 410 were the V8S.

TVR got back to building traditional sports cars with the convertible S range. It was classed as an entry level machine, specifically aimed at those who had turned their backs on TVRs because they saw them as too fast and certainly over-priced. Being a good chunk less expensive than the previous 350i model, sales of the S1 started to pick up.

resemblance to the earlier M series, but it was actually new from the ground up – apart from the door handles, that is. The company had not yet embarked on its own engine programme, so power was provided by Ford's 2.8-litre pushrod V6, more commonly found in the Granada, Capri and Sierra. This was front mounted and it drove the rear wheels through the Ford five-speed gearbox and final drive.

Following TVR tradition, the backbone chassis was a multi-tubular construction, in this case with outriggers, the steel tubes being plastic-coated for longevity. The body shell was a one-piece glassfibre moulding, the front end, bonnet and wings being a separate unit that hinged forwards for engine access. One clever part was the roof arrangement of this two-seat convertible. A folding framework carried a rear hood which incorporated the rear window, and into this slotted two solid roof panels that gave the wind-up side windows their upper seals. Something that

TVR S
1986

Engine type	V6, ohv
Power	150 bhp @ 5700 rpm
Bore/stroke	93.0 x 68.5 mm (3.7 x 2.1 in)
Capacity	2794cc (170.4 cu in)
Transmission	Rear drive, five gears
Wheelbase	2286 mm (90 in)
Top speed	209 kph (130 mph)

The headlights of the S1 were sculpted into the wing and an air-intake slot was added to the centre, upper part of the bonnet, to help feed fresh air to the engine compartment.

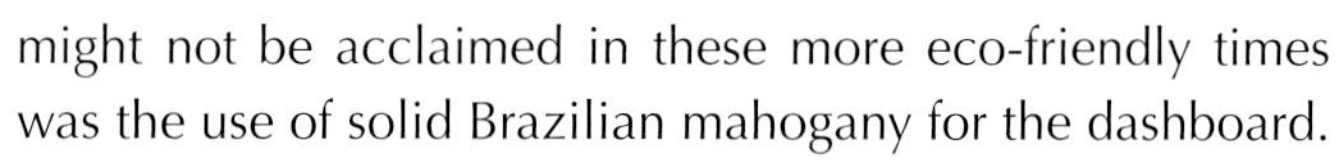

might not be acclaimed in these more eco-friendly times was the use of solid Brazilian mahogany for the dashboard.

The front suspension was by unequal-length wishbones and an anti-roll bar, with coil springs and telescopic dampers. The same spring and damper arrangement featured at the back, where semi-trailing arms provided location, aided by an anti-roll bar. The rack-and-pinion was not power-assisted, but the brakes were, with discs at the front and drums at the rear.

Although classified as producing 160 bhp by Ford, the V6 in its TVR home was catalogued as developing 150 bhp at 5700 rpm, perhaps because of exhaust system differences. Whatever the case, the S was good for 209 kph (130 mph) and it found favour with those looking for a mildy updated version of the traditional British sports car.

TVR was small enough to make modifications on the fly, so the second series of S was phased in rather than launched. By mid-1989, the S2 had definitely arrived and the principal change was that it now had the 2.9-litre version of the V6, as dictated by Ford's own production. This offered a handful of extra horsepower and a little more performance for the S, which had one or two other new features, such as revised rear suspension geometry, electric windows and new wheels.

TVRs always had plush and interesting interiors, the S1 was no exception.

These original wheels for the S1 were made by "OZ Racing" and are 15-inch diameter. Note the TVR emblem in the centre cap.

Featured in the S1 was this Ford 2.8-litre, Cologne V6 engine. This was the same unit that was being used in the Ford Capri of the period.

The S2 was phased in around 1989 and the major change was that although it still used the Ford V6 engine, it had now been increased to 2.9 litres.

By now the instrumentation and dashboard had also been revamped and there was much more padding involved, for safety reasons.

The third series was the most popular. This had bigger doors and a slightly tuned engine, exhausting in the case of the S3C – which appeared in 1991 – through a catalytic converter for the first time. A limited-slip differential was another addition and one that improved handling and roadholding.

As buyers sought more power, TVR responded in 1991 by installing the Rover V8, in tuned 4-litre form, in the S. This involved fitting Rover's own gearbox and (eventually) strengthening the now too flexible chassis and widening the track to cope with the 240 bhp that was on tap. As another nod to this prodigious output, rear discs were added to the existing front pair to complete the set and improve stopping power. Once again, there were some trim alterations, but it has often been said that no two TVRs are the same, so these were not necessarily clear identifiers. The bulging bonnet generally was one, although this had been designed for use on supercharged V6 cars for the Italian market. The SV8 was extremely fast. It could hit 100 kph (60 mph) in just 4.9 seconds and reach a top speed of nearly 241 kph (150 mph).

There was one other S road car, which was a hybrid. The S4 combined the chassis of the V8 with the V6 engine and retained the flat bonnet. Despite a hefty price premium on the V8, the V6 option was not a popular one and only a handful of cars were sold thus equipped.

S production finally came to an end in 1994. Sales had never taken off – as might have been hoped – to push TVR into a new league, but this model brought much needed income at a vital stage in the company's history. A few more than 2600 cars were sold, around 400 of them V8s.

The S3 was the most popular of the S series cars and sold the most examples. One noticeable change were the doors, which were made longer to help exit and entry to the car. Seen here is an SC, which was a post-catalytic converter model with modified engine.

An interesting view of the S2, showing the collapsed hood. Two panels are removed at the centre of the roof and stored in the small boot area. The rear section of the hood can be folded back, or if need be remain in the upright position. The dashboard looks like it could be wood, but in fact is metal with a wood effect.

Vauxhall Prince Henry

Vauxhall's Prince Henry can lay justifiable claim to being the world's first true sports car. The company had been responsible for some fairly mundane machinery before it took on a talented young engineer called Laurence Pomeroy. His first opportunity to shine came when he stood in for a holidaying chief engineer and designed a new 20 hp car for the RAC 2000-mile Trial of 1908, to which the management had committed itself. That car pulverised the opposition and similar cars were soon taking victories and breaking records far and wide.

Vauxhall was quick to capitalise on these successes, putting more civilised versions of the competition car into production as the 3-litre A-type and 2-litre B-type and introducing them at the 1908 Olympia Motor Show. The new models won approval from

Manufactured by Vauxhall Motors of England, the Prince Henry, or "C" class to give it its proper designation, was made between 1911 and 1913. The one featured here is of 1911 vintage, the earliest of only nine surviving and is owned by Vauxhall Motors. It was after competing in the Prince Henry Trials, a race named after the motoring fanatic Prince Heinrich Hohenzollern of Prussia, that the "C" type acquired its name.

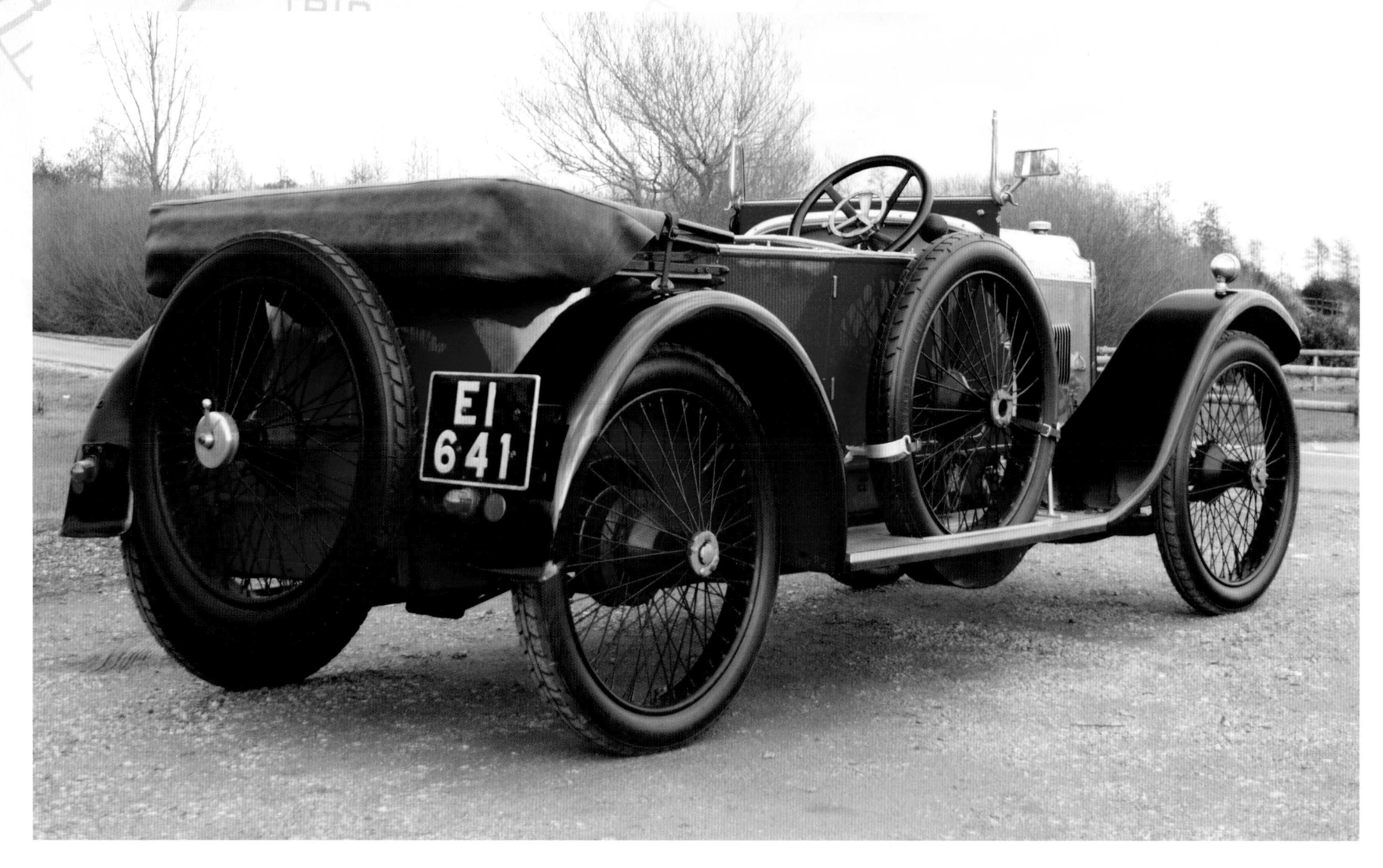

Vauxhall Prince Henry 1911

Engine type	In-line four cylinder, sv
Power	75 bhp @ 2500 rpm
Bore/stroke	90 x 120 mm (3.54 x 4.72 in)
Capacity	3053 cc (186.3 cu in)
Transmission	Rear drive, four gears
Wheelbase	2972 mm (117 in)
Top speed	121 kph (75 mph)

Vauxhall put a powerful engine (by contemporary standards) into a special short chassis and created what was Britain's first proper sports car.

press and public alike and Pomeroy's expertise was recognised in his promotion to Works Manager the following year. Vauxhall was now established as a manufacturer of desirable cars and sales reflected this.

Flushed with its success in trials and at the new Brooklands race track, the company entered the Prince Henry Trials of 1910. Prince Henry of Prussia was the brother of Kaiser Wilhelm. Married to Queen Victoria's granddaughter, he was an Anglophile and also an enthusiastic motorist. He had inaugurated the trials bearing his name in 1908, in order to discover the best touring car of the day.

Pomeroy was tasked with designing a new car to fit the regulations. A new sturdy but relatively lightweight chassis was drawn up and constructed. It carried a live rear axle and a front beam, both of which were located on rugged semi-elliptic leaf springs (there were no dampers at this stage). Only the rear wheels had brakes.

Experiments were carried out with overhead-valve engines, but these proved to be disappointing. The engines were unreliable and, in any case, they did not produce the kind of power that had been hoped for. By the time of the Prince Henry Trials, Pomeroy had settled for a tuned 60 bhp version of the 3-litre side-valve four used in the A-type. Despite its valve arrangement, this was advanced in other ways, not least in

The Prince Henry model combined the crafted coachwork of the Edwardian car with much better performance than the average touring car, appealing to the rich, gentleman racer – a market which Vauxhall cultivated at the time.

The dashboard on this 1911 model is comprehensive and classy.

The car was generally delivered with the chassis and mechanicals only, after which the customer would chose his specific bodywork from a selection of coachbuilders of the time. Interior trim could be very sumptuous and certainly leather was generally very prominent, as seen here.

having five crankshaft bearings. The engine drove the rear wheels through a leather-faced clutch and a four-speed gearbox which lacked the modern sophistication of synchromesh. A smooth and elegant doorless four-seat tourer body was added to the frame, and it was topped off by a distinctive, sharply pointed radiator.

The Vauxhall team came away empty handed from that event, largely because other teams had applied a liberal interpretation to the rules governing the configuration of participating vehicles. However, all three cars finished, two of them without making a stop, and it was not long before what was officially the C-type was available in a roadgoing incarnation and known, informally at first, as the Prince Henry. There were several more competitive forays to cement the reputation of the finest Vauxhall so far. The

This is the very efficient three-door Sports Torpedo body produced by Hoskison of Birmingham.

Principal distinguishing feature of the Prince Henry Vauxhall was the V-pointed radiator top tank with flutes. These flutes were to be a Vauxhall feature until after the Second World War.

The 4-litre Prince Henry model shown, was produced with Helle-Shore multiplate clutch, which used eleven steel plates and ten copper.

Steering column levers shown, gave the driver the option of remotely adjusting the magneto "ADV/RET", the carburettor mixture "Strong/Weak" and the engine speed by hand throttle – "Fast/Slow".

original Trials, together with further adventures such as beating a train from Melbourne to Adelaide in Australia, did no harm to sales, although the Prince Henry was not cheap, being priced at £580 with a tourer body.

In its 3-litre form, the new Vauxhall was capable of 121 kph (75 mph) or so. This would have been a frightening rate in lesser machines, but the Prince Henry was surprisingly competent in its handling, even if its brakes left something to be desired. As if that were not enough, the engine was enlarged to 4 litres in 1913, by increasing the bore and stroke size. It now produced 75 bhp, which added a little more to the maximum speed, albeit with more comfort for passengers within the available bodies.

In fact, the Prince Henry was not long-lived. However, it provided the foundations for the 30/98, which first appeared in 1913 and then returned to production after the First World War to give Vauxhall a foothold in the sporting market of the Vintage period. This was, in effect, a more civilised version of the Prince Henry, with an even bigger engine and such niceties as suspension dampers and – eventually – front-wheel brakes.

The Prince Henry itself was made only until 1913, but both its and Vauxhall's reputation was firmly established. In this era of hand-built cars, about 50 3-litre Prince Henrys were built, along with another 140 containing the larger engine.

The scuttle panel, now known as a dashboard, gave important information to the driver. This included (left to right) Petrol tank air pressure reading, Oil pressure gauge, Amp meter reading and Volt meter reading. The centre switch is the engine magneto On/Off and the six toggle switches gave individual control of the lights.The top brass plate shows maker's name, car number and serial number.

INDEX

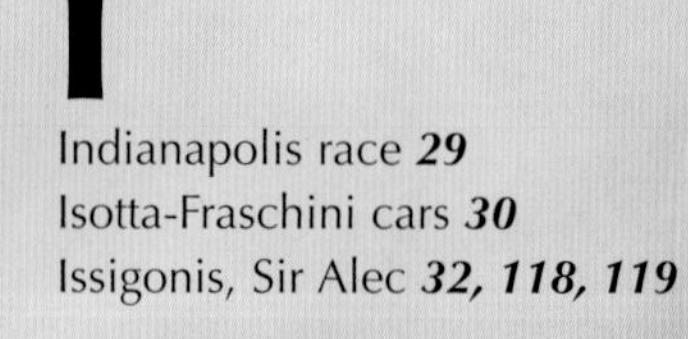

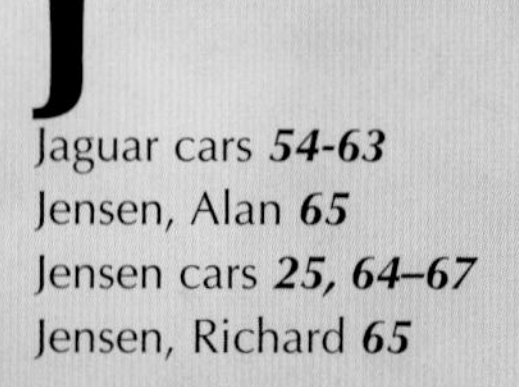

K

L

M

N

O

P

R

S

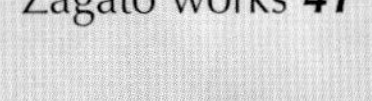

T

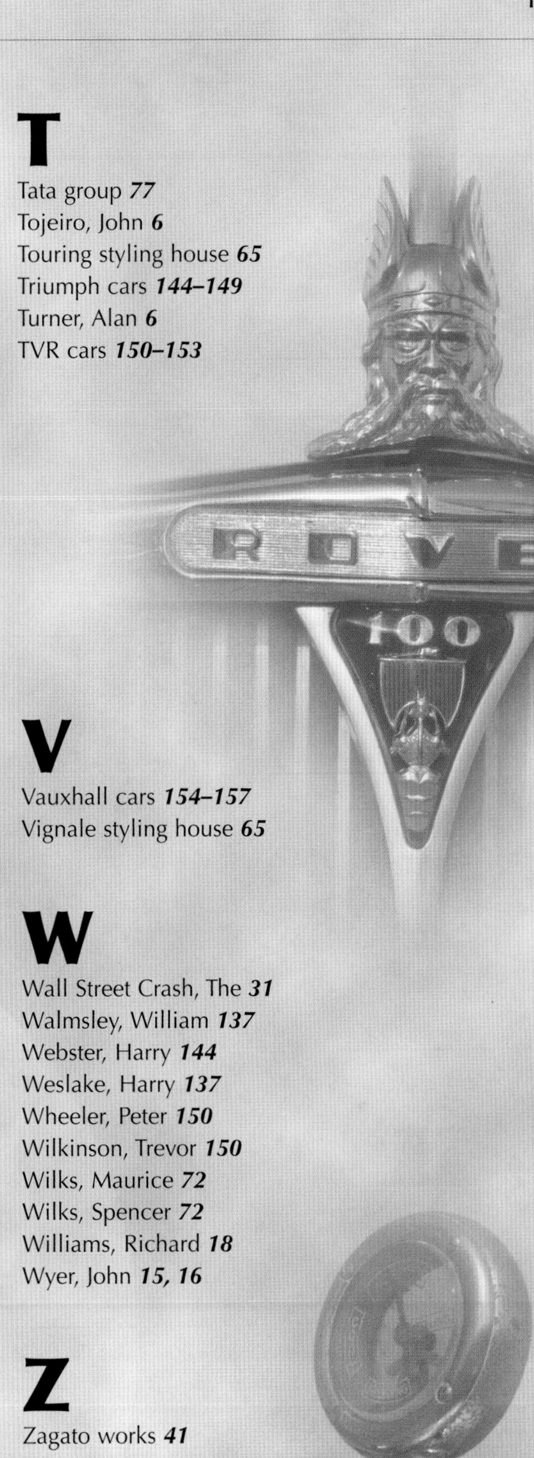

V

W

Z

ACKNOWLEDGEMENTS

The Author and Publisher would like to thank the following people and organisations for their kind help and contribution:

The Heritage Motor Centre, Gaydon, Warwickshire, England

AC Owners' Club Cobra Registrar – Robin Stainer

Sam Roberts, Editor/Archivist, Ford Y & C Model Register, Andover, England
www.fordyandcmodelregister.co.uk

Lotus 7 Register
www.lotus7register.co.uk

Club Lotus
www.club-lotus.co.uk

Lotus Drivers Club
www.LotusDriversClub.org.uk

C M Booth collection of 3-wheeler Morgans, Rolvenden, Kent, England
www.morganmuseum.org.uk

The Morgan Sports Car Club Ltd., Dudley, West Midlands, England
www.mscc.uk.com

Lagonda Club, Bristol, England
www.lagonda-club.com

Jensen Owners Club

Rover P4 Drivers Guild
www.roverp4dg.org.uk; chairman@roverp4dg.org.uk;
membership-secretary@roverp4dg.org.uk

Riley RM Club
www.rileyrmclub.org.uk

MG Owners' Club, Swavesey, Cambridge, England

Jaguar Drivers Club

CMC Classic Cars – Jaguar specialists – Bridgnorth, Shropshire, England

Sunbeam, Talbot, Alpine Register (STAR)

TVR Car Club, Newport, Shropshire, England

Caterham Midlands Ltd., Leicester, England

Vauxhall Owners Club 1903–57

A special thanks goes out to all those owners who so kindly turned out to have their car photographed come wind, rain, sun and even snow.